15
SECRETS
to a
WONDERFUL
LIFE

15
SECRETS
to a
WONDERFUL
LIFE

Mastering the Art of Positive Living

MICHAEL YOUSSEF, PhD

NEW YORK BOSTON NASHVILLE

Unless otherwise noted, scripture is taken from the HOLY BIBLE, NEW INTERNATIONAL VERSION® (NIV). Copyright © 1973, 1978, 1984 International Bible Society. Used by permission of Zondervan. All rights reserved.

Scripture taken from The Message (MSG). Copyright 1993, 1994, 1995, 1996, 2000, 2001, 2002. Used by permission of NavPress Publishing Group.

FaithWords
Hachette Book Group USA
237 Park Avenue
New York, NY 10017

Visit our Web site at www.faithwords.com.

Printed in the United States of America

First Edition: March 2008
10 9 8 7 6 5 4 3 2 1

FaithWords is a division of Hachette Book Group USA, Inc. The FaithWords name and logo is a trademark of Hachette Book Group USA, Inc.

Library of Congress Cataloging-in-Publication Data
Youssef, Michael.
   15 secrets to a wonderful life : mastering the art of positive living / Michael Youssef.—1st ed.
      p. cm.
   ISBN-13: 978-0-446-57956-8
   ISBN-10: 0-446-57956-4
   1. Christian life. I. Title. II. Title: Fifteen secrets to a wonderful life.
   BV4501.3.Y69 2008
   248.4—dc22   2007011213

To Bill and Sandra Johnson:
Thank you for your partnership in the Gospel.

CONTENTS

ACKNOWLEDGMENTS

Any book, and this one is no exception, is the product of many people's hard work. Several people deserve a special expression of thanks:

The congregation of The Church of The Apostles for their great encouragement in hearing and responding to the message of this book; Tricia Erickson, my research assistant, for patiently working on the manuscript; Jim Denney for organizing my thoughts better than I can; and, above all, Gary Terashita of FaithWords for believing that this book will be my best yet. I believe him!

Positive Thinking—*or Positive* Living?

Once upon a time, there was an American corporation that earned over $100 billion in a single year. More than twenty thousand people were employed by this company, and thousands of retirees and wage earners had their life savings invested there. *Fortune* magazine named it "America's Most Innovative Company" for six years in a row.

At the end of 2001, the world was stunned to learn that this company was a house of cards, propped up by fraudulent accounting schemes. The company filed for Chapter 11 protection—then the biggest bankruptcy in U.S. history. Thousands of employees lost their jobs and countless investors lost their retirement funds. Company stock, once valued at over ninety dollars a share, plummeted to as little as thirty cents a share.

That company was called Enron, and the head of the company was Kenneth Lay—one of the world's leading proponents of positive thinking.

Mr. Lay rose from poverty to become a self-made millionaire. Along the way, he won the Horatio Alger Award, which was created by the leader of the positive-thinking movement, Dr. Norman Vincent Peale. The Horatio Alger Award recognizes people who have gone from rags to riches through "the power of positive thinking."

In May 2006, Ken Lay was convicted on ten felony corruption counts. Before his sentence could be imposed, he died of a heart attack.

Writing in the *Washington Post* (July 6, 2006, page D1), Steven Pearlstein concluded that much of the blame for the Enron disaster could be traced to Kenneth Lay's excessive reliance on positive thinking. "The remarkable rise and tragic fall of Ken Lay," Pearlstein wrote, "is really a story about a man whose optimism was finally outrun by reality. Early on, he found he could succeed by putting the best face on things, stretching the truth, dismissing the doubts of naysayers. But in the end, those habits became his undoing."

How ironic! For more than fifty years, ever since Dr. Norman Vincent Peale published his 1952 best seller, *The Power of Positive Thinking*, we've been told that positive thinking is the key to success. Yet Ken Lay's overreliance on positive thinking helped produce one of the worst failures in business history.

Is this possible? Could there actually be a dark side to the power of positive thinking?

The Negative Power of Positive Thinking

Dr. Jimmie Holland, a psychiatrist at Memorial Sloan-Kettering Cancer Center in New York, warns against what she calls "the tyranny of positive thinking." In her book *The Human Side of*

Cancer, she describes how cancer patients sometimes come to her for counseling after being told by friends, "Your negative attitude caused your cancer." Dr. Holland says that many of these people who are facing a life-or-death medical crisis are often made to feel guilty—as if they have caused their own disease!

Dr. Holland adds that it's normal for cancer patients to feel sad, anxious, and worried. It's unrealistic to think a person can be positive all the time—and especially a person who is going through chemotherapy or radiation treatments. Yet, that is exactly what the "positive attitude police" often demand. Their "blame the victim" mentality shows how an overzealous focus on "the power of positive thinking" can sometimes produce a negative effect on human lives.[1]

Please understand, I'm not condemning cheerful, positive people—far from it. As followers of Jesus Christ, we have every reason to be joyful and optimistic. But we need to recognize there are limitations to the power of positive thinking. One of the biggest problems with positive thinking is that it's difficult to maintain our optimism through times of intense trial. In tough times, we have to repeatedly psych ourselves up in order to maintain our positive attitude.

If you listen carefully to the preaching of the power of positive thinking, you discover that it requires.

- constant self-motivation
- constant self-elevation
- constant self-affirmation.

It requires you to continually remind yourself, "I *can* do this! I *can* achieve this! I! I! I!"

What I'm telling you here is not theory. This is what people actually say to themselves in an effort to maintain a positive attitude. I know. I've tried the power of positive thinking myself—and I can tell you it may seem to work for a while, but it doesn't work over time. It doesn't work in all situations. There are limits to what positive thinking can achieve in your life.

When I tried to live by the power of positive thinking, I discovered that the very act of trying to remain positive can be exhausting and discouraging. I found that I needed a lot of mental and emotional energy to keep reminding myself throughout the day: "Be positive! Be positive! Be positive!" If I lost my positive focus, even for a moment, I'd crash and burn. In time, I discovered it often took as small a thing as misplaced car keys or a nagging backache to make me lose my positive attitude.

"*There* Must *Be a Better Way to Live!*"

Another limitation of positive thinking is that simple optimism isn't enough to sustain you when you hit a wall in life. You cannot elevate yourself over a truly devastating loss or an unsolvable crisis by reciting positive affirmations over and over again.

The positive-thinking gurus will urge you to repeat to yourself, "Every day, in every way, I'm getting better and better!" That sounds wonderful—until the day comes when you realize your health is failing, your eyesight is fading, and your body is falling apart. Or: "I love and appreciate myself just as I am." A nice thought—if it weren't for all the guilt, shame, and regret we carry around inside. Or: "My life is blossoming in total perfection." What a beautiful sentiment—until we stand at the graveside of a beloved spouse, child, or parent, and life doesn't seem so perfect anymore.

We are told to repeat to ourselves, "It's okay for me to have everything I want" or "Infinite riches are now freely flowing into my life." But this kind of so-called "positive thinking" is really nothing more than selfishness mingled with wishfulness.

Or: "I am a radiant being, filled with light and love." This kind of "positive thinking" sounds dangerously close to self-deification. Or: "I am vibrantly healthy and radiantly beautiful." But over time, our health declines and beauty fades—and such affirmations begin to sound dangerously self-delusional.

The whole purpose of these self-affirming statements is to give us something to recite that will elevate our moods, energize our motivation, and prop up our self-esteem. But when negative people, negative circumstances, and negative events start wearing down our self-affirmation, we find we are spending more days down than up.

We also discover we have developed a subconscious dependence on the things propping us up. We develop an addiction to self-help books, tapes, CDs, and videos that keep us revved up and emotionally stimulated. If we don't keep getting our positive-thinking fix, we quickly slide into the dumps.

If you've been there, as I have, if you've tried all the positive affirmations, if you've struggled to keep thinking optimistic thoughts during times of trial and stress, then you know what I'm saying is true. But, my dear reader, I have great news for you! Let me tell you what I've discovered.

After trying repeatedly to practice the power of positive thinking, I finally said to myself, "There *must* be a better way to live. There *must* be a way to live positively, regardless of the circumstances of life." Then a realization came to me: if there's a better way to live, it can only come from the Word of God.

Then I was led to one of the apostle Paul's New Testament epistles, 2 Corinthians. Bible scholars tell us 2 Corinthians is the most personal of all Paul's letters. It is there Paul reveals his heart to us—and he presents to us an inspiring, instructive example of positive living.

As I was reading through 2 Corinthians in search of the secrets of positive living, I was profoundly impressed by all Paul endured for the sake of the gospel. He recounts he was beaten

with fists, beaten with rods, stoned, shipwrecked, and imprisoned. He endured hunger and thirst and many other forms of
suffering. Reading of Paul's afflictions, I wondered, *How did
Paul manage to bounce back again and again? How did he
remain positive through so many negative circumstances?*

While reading and re-reading 2 Corinthians, I grew convinced there was a vast difference between "positive thinking" and "positive living." I realized Paul did not practice "the
power of positive thinking." He was a man who lived a *positive
life* despite all the negative circumstances surrounding him,
including opposition, setbacks, and suffering. I desperately
wanted to learn Paul's secrets of positive living.

I'm sure you want to know these secrets, too. In these fifteen chapters, I will introduce you to the secrets I have discovered in 2 Corinthians—the apostle Paul's secrets for positive
living. These are the secrets for living a positive life all the
time, no matter how many problems and obstacles life may
throw at you.

These are the very secrets that continually motivated, elevated, and encouraged the apostle Paul throughout the trials
and troubles of his life. Even when all hell was breaking loose
around him, Paul remained focused on the heavenly realities.
He didn't merely *survive* his trials; he *thrived* in the midst of
them. The fifteen secrets we'll explore in this book made all
the difference in Paul's life as he walked with Christ and lived
above his circumstances.

I pray that God will imprint these fifteen principles on your
heart, and that they will revolutionize your life just as they have
revolutionized mine.

15
SECRETS
to a
WONDERFUL
LIFE

The Inflow-Outflow Equation

They call her "Amazing Grace."

2 Corinthians 1:1–14

Do you remember the classic *Star Trek* series of the 1960s? Then you undoubtedly remember Captain Kirk's blond assistant, Yeoman Rand, played by actress Grace Lee Whitney. Before appearing in *Star Trek*, Miss Whtiney had an exciting career in films and television. She worked with the biggest stars, directors, and producers in Hollywood, including Marilyn Monroe, Shirley MacLaine, Jack Lemmon, George Burns, Groucho Marx, and Billy Wilder. When she landed the continuing role of Yeoman Rand on *Star Trek*, it was an actor's dream come true—a continuing role on a weekly dramatic series, with all the wealth and fame that goes with it.

If you are a true *Star Trek* fan, then you probably know something terrible happened to Grace Lee Whitney: her

character disappeared from the series before the end of the first season. For years afterward, fans wondered why Yeoman Rand simply vanished from the bridge of the Starship *Enterprise*. After a long self-imposed silence, Miss Whitney came forward and told her story in a book called *The Longest Trek: My Tour of the Galaxy*.

One evening after a cast party on the *Star Trek* set, a studio executive invited Grace to his office for a talk. He told her he had big plans for increasing her role on the show and wanted to discuss her future. But once he had her alone in his office, he sexually assaulted her. As if the assault weren't devastating enough, Grace came back the following week to begin shooting the next episode—and was told she was being written out of the series. The producer who assaulted her didn't want her around to remind him of what he had done—so he got her fired from the show.

Even before this crisis in her professional life, Grace Lee Whitney struggled with crippling childhood memories and shame. After being assaulted and tossed off the TV series, she plunged into a deep depression. She tried to deaden her pain by binging on alcohol, drugs, and compulsive sexual behavior. She didn't merely want to stop hurting—she wanted to die. Over the next ten years, as her alcoholism and other addictions spun completely out of control, she was reduced to sitting on a curb in downtown Los Angeles, drinking cheap booze straight from the bottle.

Finally, she was admitted to a hospital, suffering from dehydration and delirium tremens. The doctor who examined her said her liver was dangerously enlarged and her esophagus was perforated from all the cheap gin she'd been drinking. "If you don't stop drinking," he told her, "you'll die."

"How long do I have?" she asked. "How many months?"

"Not months," the doctor replied. "Days."

This scared her—but Grace didn't know how to stop drinking. Alcoholism had her in an unbreakable grip.

Soon after Grace was released from the hospital, a friend invited her to a twelve-step recovery group. She was introduced to a roomful of people who admitted they were powerless against alcoholism. They lived day by day without drinking by relying on the power of God. Grace Lee Whitney never took another drink after she began her twelve-step recovery process. She remains in recovery to this day. In 1983, after two years of sobriety, Grace committed her life to Jesus Christ as her Lord and Savior.

Today, Grace Lee Whitney represents Jesus Christ at *Star Trek* conventions and in radio and TV interviews. She shares the story of what God did in her life at twelve-step recovery meetings and in women's prisons. She donates countless hours, counseling and sponsoring women with addictions. Now you see why people call her "Amazing Grace."

After suffering childhood pain, a sexual assault, and a nearly fatal addiction, Grace has received salvation, physical and emotional healing, and a new life from God. Not content to merely receive the gift of God's love, she also gives His love away to others. Grace Lee Whitney is a living example of Paul's first secret of positive living: "The Inflow-Outflow Equation."

The First Secret

In my study of Paul's second letter to the Corinthians, I found at least fifteen powerful, life-changing secrets of positive living. I would encourage you to sit down with this epistle and read it from start to finish. Bathe your mind in the truths of this great message from the apostle Paul, and I guarantee you'll find it a life-changing experience.

You cannot read this letter without being amazed at how one man could endure so many tragic and unjust experiences as Paul. He was like a boxer. Again and again, the world took its best shot at him, sometimes knocking Paul to the canvas—yet he would always get back on his feet and fight his way through each round. Paul never went down for the count. He refused to let negative people and negative circumstances keep him from going the distance for God.

Let's look briefly at the background of this letter. The city of Corinth was a major center of trade, wealth, and culture in the Roman Empire. It was also a city given over to moral depravity and the worship of Aphrodite, the Greek goddess of sexual love. The Christians in Corinth were surrounded by the same kinds of pressures and temptations surrounding us today. So the words Paul writes and the principles he shares in this letter are meant as much for you and me today as they were meant for the Christians in first-century Corinth.

Paul had a special relationship with the church in Corinth. He founded the Corinthian church around A.D. 52 or 53 (about five years before this letter was written) and he lived, preached, and ministered in that city for about eighteen months to two years. From Corinth, he moved on to Ephesus in Asia Minor (modern-day Turkey). While he was in Ephesus, word came to Paul of problems in the Corinthian church. He wrote the letter we know as 1 Corinthians in order to address those problems.

Later, Paul left Ephesus and went to the region of Troas in northwest Asia Minor (Troas was named after the ancient city of Troy, which was located in that region). After spending time in Troas, Paul journeyed into Macedonia, where he met with Titus, his partner in ministry, who had just come from Corinth. During his journey from Troas, Paul suffered great persecution and opposition, and he was weary and discouraged by the time he stopped in Macedonia. So when Titus came with good news from Corinth, the apostle Paul was greatly encouraged.

So Paul told the Corinthians:

"For when we came into Macedonia, this body of ours had no rest, but we were harassed at every turn—conflicts on the outside, fears within. But God, who comforts the downcast, comforted us by the coming of Titus, and not only by his coming but also by the comfort you had given him. He told us about your longing for me, your deep sorrow, your ardent concern for me, so that my joy was greater than ever."

(2 Corinthians 7:5-7)

However, not all the news from Corinth was good. Sometime after Paul's last visit, the Corinthian church was infiltrated by people who spread lies about Paul while preaching a false gospel. Paul refers to them as "false apostles, deceitful workmen, masquerading as apostles of Christ" (2 Cor. 11:13). They opposed Paul's work and caused him considerable grief and suffering. We will learn more about these false teachers in later chapters.

In Paul's second epistle to the Corinthians, the apostle reveals his inner anguish and frustration, his discouragement and temptations, his loneliness and weaknesses. He describes how he was beaten, criticized, and falsely accused for the sake of Jesus Christ. Most important of all, he reveals to us the power of God working in the midst of his pain. In this letter, the apostle Paul opens up his life for us to see—and he reveals to us how God's power is at work in the midst of trials and afflictions.

We begin our study of Paul's fifteen secrets of positive living with "The Inflow-Outflow Equation." Paul writes:

Praise be to the God and Father of our Lord Jesus Christ, the Father of compassion and the God of all comfort, who comforts us in all our troubles, so that we can comfort those in any trouble with the comfort we ourselves have received from God. For just as the sufferings of Christ flow over into our lives, so also through Christ our comfort overflows. If we are distressed, it is for your comfort and salvation; if we are comforted, it is for your comfort, which produces in you patient endurance of the same sufferings we suffer. And our hope for you is firm, because we know that just as you share in our sufferings, so also you share in our comfort.

(2 Corinthians 1:3-7)

In these verses, there is one word Paul uses nine times, and it is the key word of this passage: "comfort." Paul speaks of comfort in terms of giving and receiving, and hence The Inflow-Outflow Equation. Inflow is only the first half of the equation.

First, the Inflow

Because we live in this evil and fallen world, we face problems and troubles of various kinds: illness, sorrow, loss, opposition, injustice, difficult people, strained or broken relationships, disappointments, disillusionment, helplessness, hopelessness, and despair. If you have not faced these kinds of trials yet, you will. Affliction is an inevitable part of life.

Satan wants to use painful experiences to discourage and defeat us. He wants to stop us from accomplishing great things for God. He wants to keep us from having an impact on the world for Christ. In the Old Testament and the New Testament and in our daily lives, we see that one of Satan's favorite strategies is to use tragedy as a weapon against God's people.

When you are under attack by Satan, it will do little good to prop yourself up with "the power of positive thinking." Satan can outthink you every time. But here's the good news: Whenever you hit one of life's brick walls, God is there. His infinite power is available to you. His weapons are far more powerful than the weapons of Satan.

We can't always feel God's presence—but He is always dynamically involved in our lives. He is ready to soothe your wounds, fill your emptiness, and mend your brokenness. He is ready to restore your confidence and renew your hopes and dreams.

God never promised us a life free from trials and troubles, but He repeatedly promises to be with us, comforting and strengthening us in the midst of our problems. We see this truth dramatically demonstrated in the life and letters of the apostle Paul. One fact comes through clearly in this letter: If ever there was a man who struggled, who faced persecution and opposition, and who had every reason to be resentful, angry, discouraged, and pessimistic, it was the apostle Paul—yet Paul was never defeated by his trials. Instead, he shouts to us, "Praise be to the God and Father of our Lord Jesus Christ, the Father of compassion and the God of all comfort, who comforts us in all our troubles" (2 Cor. 1:3–4a).

Is this the same apostle Paul who was beaten with fists and wooden rods? Who was stoned almost to death not once but several times? Who was shipwrecked and falsely imprisoned and lied about and opposed by false teachers? Who endured hunger and thirst for the sake of the gospel? Shouldn't he be bitter and pessimistic about his life?

Yet, Paul's response is a shout of triumph, praise, and thanksgiving that "the God of all comfort" has comforted him in all of his troubles. Had you and I suffered what Paul suffered, we might not be so full of praise. We would hire an attorney to sue everyone who lied about us and falsely imprisoned us. We'd demand our constitutional rights. We'd send out mass mailings, protesting our unfair treatment. We'd put up a Web site on the Internet, explaining our innocence.

But Paul's response is one of praise and thanksgiving to the God of all comfort. He says, in effect, "I'm not focused on the negative circumstances in my life. I'm focused on the God of *all* comfort, who comforts me in *all* my troubles and afflictions.

I'm focused on the Friend who, as Proverbs 18:24 says, 'sticks closer than a brother.'" As Paul wrote in another New Testament letter, "If God is for us, who can be against us? He who did not spare his own Son, but gave him up for us all—how will he not also, along with him, graciously give us all things?" (Rom. 8:31b-32).

As long as the God of all comfort is with me, no one can get me down. Problems can't cripple my faith. Financial setbacks can't cause me to despair. Neither illness nor injury can hinder me. False accusers have no power over me. Troubled relationships can't lessen my resolve. I refuse to allow even a bad hair day to ruin my demeanor. Why? Because the God of *all* comfort continually comforts me in *all* my afflictions. I continually receive an inflow of comfort from the Lord my God.

You may say, "But I'm not experiencing this inflow you speak of. I'm hurting, and I'm not being comforted. Why don't I receive this inflow?"

I can't judge your heart, but I do want to offer one possible explanation for why you may not be experiencing an inflow of comfort from God: It may be you are using a "do it yourself" approach to finding comfort for your afflictions. The "do it yourself" approach says, "I can do it! I can do it! I can do it!" The truth is: no, you can't!

Your business has failed. Or your romance has ended. Or a friend has betrayed you. Or your teenage child has turned away from you. Or a loved one has died. You're trying to keep your chin up. You're trying to prop up your spirits and keep going on. Chances are you're gritting your teeth so hard your jaws are ready to crack.

I know how it feels. I have been hurt and I have tried the "do it yourself" approach myself—and every time I've tried it, I've failed. You can't pull yourself up into the air by tugging on your shoelaces. By the same token, you can't comfort yourself in your own afflictions. You need God to lift you, to put His loving arms around you and comfort you.

Today, you can know the comfort of God. He's not the God of *some* comfort; He's the God of *all* comfort. He will comfort you—not just in *some* of your afflictions, but in *all* your afflictions. Not just occasionally, but *always*. Not just in certain areas of life, but in *all* areas of life.

That's why Paul says in 2 Corinthians 1:5, "For just as the sufferings of Christ flow over into our lives, so also through Christ our comfort overflows." In other words, Paul is saying, "Make my day. Bring on the sufferings of Christ. The more afflictions come my way, the more comfort I experience from God! And the more comfort I experience from God, the more His comfort overflows from my life to the lives of others."

This is the "inflow" half of The Inflow-Outflow Equation: as we experience trouble and trials, God's comfort flows into our lives.

Next, the Outflow

Paul begins describing the inflow with these words: "Praise be to the God and Father of our Lord Jesus Christ, the Father of compassion and the God of all comfort, who comforts us in all our troubles" (2 Cor. 1:3–4a).

But Paul's sentence doesn't end there. Had Paul ended his statement at this point, he would not have given us the whole truth. He goes on to say God comforts us in our troubles "so that we can comfort those in any trouble with the comfort we ourselves have received from God" (2 Cor. 1:4b). In other words, God comforts us so we can give His comfort away to others.

If you truly want to experience the God of all comfort, who comforts us in all our afflictions, there must not only be an inflow. There must also be an outflow.

The inflow of God's comfort and blessing is yours for the asking. The fulfillment of His promises is sure and certain. You need never doubt the availability of the inflow. But there must also be an outflow. In order for the inflow of God's blessing to take hold in your life, for His comfort to meet your need in times of affliction, there must be an outflow.

The Bible speaks of sowing and reaping. Jesus said, "From everyone who has been given much, much will be demanded" (Luke 12:48); and also, "With the measure you use, it will be measured to you" (Matt. 7:2). So if you give a little thimbleful, don't expect to receive buckets in return. But if you give freely, cheerfully, and abundantly—open your front door wide. A heavenly dump truck is on its way to pour out God's blessings upon you!

But be careful about the attitude with which you give. Some people view God's blessings as an end in themselves. They receive a blessing from God and they say, "That's what life is all about—receiving blessings from the Lord." They think God's ultimate purpose in time and space is to shower them with blessings.

But that's not what life is all about, according to the Scriptures. Paul tells us the Christian life is to be lived according to The Inflow-Outflow Equation: first, there's an inflow of comfort and blessing from God into our lives; then there is an outflow of comfort and blessing from our lives to others.

The apostle Paul sees it as a matter of stewardship. God has entrusted a measure of comfort to Paul—but Paul is not supposed to merely keep that comfort for his own use. God intended to make Paul a channel of comfort and blessing to the people around him. To Paul, it would have been a sin for him to receive blessings from God only to bottle them up and put them on a shelf. Blessings and comfort are meant to be shared.

A Tale of Two Seas

There are two major bodies of water in Israel. One is the Sea of Galilee. It's a beautiful, untainted sea, and its water is clean and sparkling. Why? Because the water flows from the slopes of Mount Hermon, down into the Sea of Galilee—and then the water flows out again via the River Jordan. Millions of people, both Arabs and Jews, are blessed by the outflow from the Sea of Galilee. The sea is fed by an inflow and it feeds the River Jordan with its outflow.

The second major body of water in Israel is the Dead Sea. The name of the Dead Sea tells the story: the water flows into the Dead Sea, but it does not flow out. Scientists tell us the Dead Sea is the deepest hypersaline (supersalty) lake in the world. The Dead Sea is located at the lowest point on earth (1,371 feet below sea level), so its waters can't flow out. The Jordan River flows in—and its waters simply collect and evaporate in the basin of the Dead Sea.

Because of the high salt content, it's easy to float on the Dead Sea—but nothing can live in that brine. In fact, those who step into its waters say it has an unpleasant oily feel and it stings the eyes. The Dead Sea is shrinking year by year—drying up and becoming increasingly salty. Eventually, if nothing is done to prevent it, the Dead Sea will dry up completely, leaving behind a broad plain of crystallized salt.

What clearer picture could we have of the life that receives great inflow but which experiences no outflow? God wants us to be sparkling, life-giving Seas of Galilee. Tragically, all too many of us are Dead Seas—all inflow and no outflow. Our lives are drying up, shrinking, and devoid of life. Those who live by The Inflow-Outflow Equation know that the outflow of comfort and blessing must keep pace with the inflow—or the result is death.

The most positive people on God's earth are people who

live by The Inflow-Outflow Equation. I've known a number of people who live by this principle, and I'm sure you know such people as well. It doesn't matter how negative their circumstances, they live positive lives and are a blessing to everyone they meet. They may be afflicted with poverty. They may suffer from chronic pain or cancer. They may be bound to a sickbed or a wheelchair. Yet, a few moments with them feels like a fresh breeze from heaven.

Paul was that kind of person. He wrote that God "comforts us in all our troubles, *so that* we can comfort those in any trouble with the comfort we ourselves have received from God." Notice the clause: "so that." It's called a "purpose clause." Paul is saying he received comfort from God for a specific and important purpose. What purpose? It is *so that* Paul might share the comfort of God with other people who are suffering.

Spiritually Fit—or Spiritually Obese?

Here's an illustration of The Inflow-Outflow Equation from my own life: I get a lot of exercise. I work out five and even six days a week. I run. I pump iron. I do everything I can to stay in shape. I avoid junk food and try to eat only good, nourishing, healthy food. I have been trying to eat a healthy diet and exercise regularly for quite a while—but I wasn't always so health conscious.

I only became serious about my health after my doctor examined me one day and said, "Michael, you are digging your own grave with a knife and fork. If you keep living that way— eating too much junk food and not exercising—you're going to get sick. You're on track to develop diabetes or have a major heart attack." Those words scared me—and I decided to get serious about my physical health.

Now, if you've ever seen me in person, you know I'm no Superman. Even exercising and eating right as I do today, I am not likely to be mistaken for an Olympic athlete. So I wonder what I would look like if I was still eating junk food and never working out. I would probably be as big as a house. But because I exercise and eat healthy food, I feel better today than I ever felt before.

There was a time, back in the days before I was exercising, when I would huff and puff while climbing a single flight of stairs. I could hardly catch my breath. Why? Because I was ignoring The Inflow-Outflow Equation in my personal health. I was experiencing an inflow of calories in all of the food I was eating—but I was not experiencing an outflow of calories through vigorous exercise. The abundance of my inflow, which was not balanced by any outflow through exercise, was producing weakness and death in my physical life. Only when my outflow began to keep pace with my inflow, did I become physically healthy and strong.

You may be physically fit, but if there is no outflow to match the inflow of blessing you receive from God, you are becoming spiritually obese and unhealthy. It breaks my heart to say this, but I'm convinced it's true: The church of Jesus Christ is filled with believers who are spiritually obese. Their souls are sick and unhealthy because there is no outflow of blessing from their lives. There is much coming in, but very little going out. They receive and receive and receive some more—but where is the blessing flowing from their lives to the work of the Kingdom of God?

One reason some people have no outflow to match their inflow is they lack faith and trust in God. They are reluctant to give because they don't trust God to bless them tomorrow as He's blessed them today. So they hoard God's blessing. They bottle it up. And in the process of hoarding what God has given them, they become spiritually obese.

I have never known a positive person who only received blessing from God. I have never met a positive person whose outflow did not match his inflow. I have never met a positive person who was only a taker. Positive people are unselfish and giving people. Their lives are a constant blessing to others. Their lives overflow with praise to God, service to the Kingdom, and ministry to other people.

Can your outflow ever exceed your inflow? Absolutely not! You can't outgive God. Whatever blessing and comfort you give to others can never be greater than the blessing and comfort God has poured into your life.

How do you receive God's blessing and comfort? There's no mystery to it. Simply ask—and you shall receive. The blessings of God are yours for the asking. If you are not receiving blessing from God, it's not because He is withholding. It's because you have closed yourself up. God longs to give you His blessing and comfort. He has promised it to you in His Word. As Isaiah writes, "Comfort, comfort my people, says your God. . . . He tends his flock like a shepherd: He gathers the lambs in his arms and carries them close to his heart" (Isa. 40:1, 11a).

We know the inflow of God's blessing is certain and dependable. In His Word, God has lovingly obligated Himself to bless us. So the question we must ask ourselves is: does my outflow match my inflow?

Now, I'm sure, you can readily see the dramatic difference between the power of positive thinking and the secrets of positive living. All the positive affirmations and positive self-talk in the world will not last. It will not carry you through times of affliction and suffering. But if you live in such a way that the outflow of God's blessing matches the inflow of God's blessing in your life, then you will experience a continuously positive life, even amid the most negative situations. If you let the comfort, encouragement, and ministry of God flow through you to others, you will be a positive person in all the circumstances of your life.

You may say, "But I don't have time to minister to others and encourage others. I have a very busy life." I know that. We are all busy people. I remember when our children were young and we were constantly carpooling and transporting kids from school to music lessons to Little League, and on and on. In our busy lives, we tend to think, *Oh, I have to go here. I'm obligated to do this. I have to attend that. I can't get out of all these obligations. And oh yes, I really should pencil in a little time on my schedule for ministry to others.*

We make out our budget and are careful to pay our debts on time—the mortgage, the car payment, the credit cards, the grocery bill, the cable bill, the dog food bill. "And oh yes," we remind ourselves, "we should also give a tithe, if we can spare it."

The Scriptures tell us God is to receive the firstfruits—not just of our money, but of our time and energy as well. If we would just give gratefully to God, and give Him the firstfruits, then the rest of the list would be taken care of. God will provide all the time, money, and energy we need to meet the demands of our busy lives. I can personally testify that this is true. Many other Christians can offer the same testimony.

Unfortunately, all too many Christians give God the least and the last rather than the firstfruits. Here's a true story that illustrates how many of us feel about giving to God:

Every year before Thanksgiving Day, the Butterball Turkey Talk Line receives hundreds of calls from people seeking advice on how to thaw, prepare, and roast their holiday turkey. One year, a woman called to ask if the turkey in her freezer was still good to eat. The Butterball Turkey expert asked how long the bird had been in the woman's freezer. The caller replied: "Twenty-three years." The turkey expert told her that after more than two decades in the Deepfreeze, the turkey would probably have a distinct "freezer taste," and he recommended the woman discard it and buy a new turkey at the market.

"That's what I was thinking," the woman said. "Well, we'll just donate the old turkey to the church."

Isn't that how we often view our giving to the Lord? We lavish the firstfruits and the best fruits on ourselves, and we give God our leftovers and rejects. Have you been holding onto the storehouse of tithes and offerings, blessings and comfort, time and energy that rightfully belong to God? Have you rationalized in your mind, "God knows I don't have time to be involved in a ministry. He knows I have too many bills to put Him first right now." My friend, put God first. Put your ministry to others first. Put your service to the Kingdom first—and see if the inflow of God doesn't overwhelm you.

What kind of ministry should you do? Well, start right where you live. Have you had your neighbors over for coffee and dessert and a conversation about what Jesus Christ has done in your life? Have you ever created an opportunity for witnessing at the supermarket—perhaps by letting someone go ahead of you in the checkout line? If you're a woman, have you started a book study with some of the women in your neighborhood? If you're a man, have you invited some friends out for golf or bowling or a barbecue and a chance to get acquainted and share your faith? There are countless ways to let your outflow match your inflow right in your own neighborhood.

And, of course, there are many ministries within the church: Hosting a Bible study. Teaching Sunday school. Volunteering for children's ministry. Serving the homeless. Donating time in the church office. You can even ask God to give you a vision for some ministry never before done in your church—and you can lead it. Ask God to show you some creative new ways to let your outflow match your inflow.

God is pouring out His blessing in your life, and He is looking for people who will be like the Sea of Galilee, not the Dead Sea. He wants His blessings to flow through you and on to others. Don't bottle up His abundant grace inside you. Share it with others. Take that important first step toward positive living by offering yourself in service to God and others.

God blessed you in so many ways. He's given you an education, shelter, food, health, and finances. He's blessed you with friends, relatives, loved ones, and close relationships. Have you been through trials and difficulties? Then He has blessed you with mercy and comfort.

Have you responded in gratitude to God's blessings? Or have you taken credit for all the blessings He has poured out on your life? You may have thought to yourself, "I don't owe God anything. The things I have are due to my own hard work, my own ingenuity." But who gave you the strength to work? Who gave you the ingenuity to achieve what you have?

God has blessed you, my friend, in order to draw you to Himself. When He blesses you, He invites you to come to Him and accept Him, to repent of your sins and receive Jesus as Savior and Lord of your life. If you have never made that decision before, you can do so right now, even before you finish reading this page.

"I made a pact with God"

Writer Benjamin Hughes, of the BaltimoreStories.com Web site, tells the story of Kevin Anderson. Several years ago, Anderson worked as a liaison for international affairs at the Pentagon in Washington, D.C. One fall morning, he overslept and was late for work. The date: September 11, 2001.

If Kevin Anderson had not overslept that morning, he would have been in the section of the Pentagon that took a direct hit when terrorists flew an American Airlines Boeing 757 into the building at over four hundred miles per hour. Kevin Anderson believes his life was spared for a reason. God blessed him, he says, so he could be a blessing to inner-city kids.

Anderson retired from the military and took a position with the Department of Agriculture. Today, in his spare time, he coaches youth basketball at a YMCA in inner-city Baltimore. And he doesn't just teach basketball to those kids. He talks to them about life—his life and their lives. "He uses lessons in basketball to carry over into everyday life," writes Hughes. "Anderson says if a kid is late for basketball practice, then he'll be late for his job. He wants his players to treat playing basketball for him like a job."

Working with youth has given Kevin Anderson a few scary moments. For example, there was the time a disagreement erupted on the basketball court and a young teen pulled a gun on him. Anderson was able to convince the gun-wielding teen that he was there to help—and the teen eventually became a friend and supporter. "Kids will work for you," Anderson says, "if you show you will work for them."

Before his brush with death on 9/11, Kevin Anderson led a less-than-exemplary life, which included drugs and fighting. Now he leads a new life. "I made a pact with God to stay off drugs," Anderson says today. "God has blessed me. And I'm out here trying to bless others."[1]

Kevin Anderson is blessed to be alive after the 9/11 terrorist attack—and he lives to share his blessings with others. That's what it means to live by The Inflow-Outflow Equation.

Claiming the Priceless Deposit

Let me give you a parable.

Imagine you have a house to sell. Your whole future depends on the sale of that house. But there's a problem: The house is falling apart. Because the house is in such deplorable condition, no one bothers to look inside. People drive by the front of your house, slow down for two or three seconds—then speed away.

The real estate agent says, "You need to do something about your house if you wish to sell it. In its present state, your house is worthless. No one in his right mind would buy a house that's falling apart."

You know your house is in shambles—but you can't afford to fix it. The longer your house sits unsold, the more money you lose. All your net worth is tied up in your house and there is

2 Corinthians 1:15–2:4

nothing you can do about it. You face financial ruin, and there's no solution to your problem.

But then, when you reach the very depths of despair . . .

Someone shows up and says, "I want to buy your house. Not only that, but I insist on paying you *more* than your asking price. What's more, I insist on giving you a cash deposit right on the spot."

This is unbelievable! It's too good to be true! Is it a hoax? Is it a dream? This kind of good luck just doesn't happen! So you ask, "How much of a deposit are you willing to put down? Ten percent?"

"Oh no," the buyer says. "More than that."

"Twenty percent?"

"*Much* more!"

"Fifty percent? You certainly wouldn't go *that* high!"

"*Much* higher! I'm going to give you a *one hundred percent deposit* on your house!"

So you agree to accept this unbelievable offer before the buyer comes to his senses! He hands you the cash—100 percent of your asking price. Then he says, "One day soon, I'll come back to close escrow and take possession of the house."

Now, I ask you: What emotions would you feel at this point? Would you feel joy? Excitement? Gratitude? Would you have a sense of anticipation as you await the day the buyer returns to close on the house? Of course you would!

And what if you had some problem in the meantime? What if you discovered a leak in the roof? Or some backed-up plumbing? Or a crack in the foundation? Would it ruin your day? Of course not. Your worries are over. The house is sold! The money is in your pocket. No matter what happens to the house, it's not your problem. You already have the entire deposit, paid in full. You're just waiting for the buyer to return and close escrow.

When you possess the total as a deposit, you have nothing to worry about.

As I've already noted, this is a parable. No parable of mine could ever convey God's limitless generosity in sending His Son to pay our debt of sin. But I hope that this analogy will give you at least a glimpse of the spiritual reality Paul describes for us in the next few verses of 2 Corinthians.

Here, Paul tells us we have received God's deposit—100 percent of the purchase price—for our salvation. It has been paid in full. And because we have received the full payment for our debt of sin as a deposit, the problems and afflictions of this life need not throw us into despair. We have a different perspective on life than those who have no hope of salvation.

Though we await the day the Lord will return and close escrow on our salvation, we have already received the 100 percent deposit. No amount of suffering or affliction can ever take it away from us. Here is how the apostle Paul explains this principle: "Now it is God who makes both us and you stand firm in Christ. He anointed us, set his seal of ownership on us, and put his Spirit in our hearts as a deposit, guaranteeing what is to come" (2 Cor. 1:21–22).

Paul says God has "anointed us, set his seal of ownership on us, and put his Spirit in our hearts as a deposit, guaranteeing what is to come." The Spirit is the 100 percent deposit. We have received it all! True, the "sale" will not be "closed" until we reach our eternal destination—but the deposit has been paid in full. It is already ours.

This amazing deposit, which was paid on the cross by the Lord Jesus Christ, became the all-consuming focus of Paul's life. The apostle Paul lived his entire life in view of having received this marvelous deposit. It was the knowledge of this guarantee of salvation that gave Paul the ability to endure affliction with patience and perseverance. For Paul, the 100 percent deposit for his eternal redemption became:

- his all-consuming thought
- his all-motivating drive
- the single most important fact in his life.

You and I have received this same deposit if we have placed our trust in Jesus Christ as our Lord and Savior. Here we see the second secret of positive living: the precious deposit we have received through Jesus Christ. We must not only *know* the deposit is ours, but we must *claim* that precious deposit in every circumstance of our lives.

When trials and troubles come our way, we can say with the apostle Paul:

> God has affirmed His promise to me with His eternal and abiding "Yes!" He enables me to stand firm in Christ, no matter how much opposition I face, no matter how much suffering and affliction may come my way. God has anointed me and has set His seal of ownership upon my life! He has put His Spirit in my heart as a 100 percent deposit on my salvation, guaranteeing that I am an heir of eternal life and a child of the King.
>
> *(see 2 Corinthians 1:18-22)*

Does this mean it's easy to endure mistreatment and suffering? No. Paul did not enjoy his sufferings, nor was he indifferent to them. No one could possibly feel good about being stoned or flogged. No one could enjoy being slandered and falsely accused. No one could remain indifferent to gnawing sensations of hunger and thirst. Paul suffered all these forms of affliction and more—but he was not defeated by them!

Affliction didn't weaken his faith. When he was mistreated, he responded with patience and perseverance, knowing he had already received God's 100 percent deposit on his salvation. Nothing in the world could rob him of it. He claimed the deposit as his own.

Who Will Swallow Gravel for You?

Have you ever experienced what Paul faced in Corinth? Have you ever been marked for opposition by people who hated you? Or targeted by a relentless smear-and-gossip campaign? Have you ever had people follow you around and nip at your heels like one of those annoying little yapping dogs? How would you handle a situation like that?

Many people today live under similar circumstances. There are pastors under attack from factions and individuals in the church. There are business leaders under constant attack from unscrupulous people in the company. There are political leaders under relentless attack by political opponents or the news media. There are husbands constantly criticized by their wives, and wives continually berated by their husbands.

Whenever we must endure a daily barrage of criticism and abuse, it wears us down. It crushes the human spirit. When the relationship between husband and wife, or parents and children, starts to deteriorate, Christlike forgiveness departs and the home becomes a prison of resentment and misery. When a home divides into two warring factions, both sides become wary. Each person is poised and hair-triggered, just waiting for the other one to make a mistake—or anything that can be interpreted as a mistake.

John says, "Mary, you haven't worn that blue dress in a while. You should wear it to the office party tomorrow."

Mary explodes. "Are you saying I'm too fat?" she shouts. "How dare you remind me I can't fit into that blue dress anymore! Mother warned me you were cruel and insensitive! If only I'd listened to her!"

Or Ann says, "Tom, your company doesn't appreciate you enough. You should go to the boss and ask for a raise."

Tom explodes. "Oh, I know what you're *really* saying!" he shouts. "You mean I'm a lousy provider! You're saying I'm so wishy-washy I'm afraid to ask the boss for a raise! Look, I don't need you to tell me what a failure I am! Just keep out of my business and quit pushing me around!"

When Christlike forgiveness has departed, even the most innocent suggestion can be twisted into a monstrous offense. Soon both people are wary and suspicious, continually expecting the worst, and ready to pounce on any unguarded word, glance, or tone of voice. Why do we do this to each other? Because we want to prove ourselves right. We gain a perverse sense of satisfaction in saying, "I was right all along—and you're wrong."

I was born in Egypt, and in the Middle East we have a profound saying. It rhymes in the original language, but the meaning is still true and powerful in unrhymed English:

He who hates you will count your every little mistake;
But he who loves you will swallow the gravel for you.

When hatred and bitterness fill your heart, you wait for the other person to make a slip—even an innocent slip—so you have an excuse to condemn him. But when you love someone, you want to catch that person doing the right thing so you can compliment him. You will do anything for that person—even to the point of swallowing gravel.

The apostle Paul had a number of close Christian friends who loved him, who were unfailingly loyal to him, who would even swallow gravel for him. Paul names two of them in his writings—Silas and Timothy. Silas was Paul's companion during his first and second missionary journeys. Timothy was the young man Paul mentored, and whom Paul called "my true son in the faith" (1 Tim. 1:2).

But Paul also knew what it was like to have enemies—people who twisted everything he did or said and used it against him. There was a group of these enemies in Corinth. They hated Paul's apostolic authority. They hated his popularity. They hated his teaching of the gospel of Jesus Christ. They hated his strong stance for the truth. They hated everything about the apostle Paul, and they were constantly nip-nip-nipping at his heels. They spread lies about him and followed him from town to town, stirring up opposition against him.

These people were not just Paul's enemies; they were enemies of the gospel of Jesus Christ. They had a simple strategy: Destroy Paul's credibility and you undermine his teaching. Turn people against Paul and you turn people against the gospel. Their strategy was truly Satan's strategy—a strategy the devil has employed against God's people for thousands of years, and which he still employs against us today.

When you are attacked, you need some gravel swallowers in your life. But what about those who, instead of swallowing gravel, throw stones at you? What about those who rant and rave against you, who hate you because you are a Christian, and who despise you because of your witness for Christ and your moral principles? Remember that those people don't hate you for yourself. They hate the gospel. They are pawns in Satan's age-old strategy. Don't take it personally, and don't let anyone keep you from boldly living for Christ.

If you take a stand for God, people will throw (figurative) stones at you, just as they threw (literal) stones at the apostle Paul. Don't let your faith be weakened. Don't lose sight of your purpose in life. Respond with grace and perseverance, just as Paul did. Remember that you have already received God's 100 percent deposit on your salvation—and nothing can ever rob you of it. Claim it; the deposit is fully yours.

Don't Take the Bait!

Next, notice the flimsy pretext Paul's enemies used as an excuse to attack his reputation. Paul had previously sent word to the Christians in Corinth that he was planning to visit them twice. He intended to visit Corinth, then go up to Macedonia, then come back again through Corinth for a second visit. Circumstances changed, however, and Paul was forced to change his plans and visit Corinth once instead of twice. He explained it this way: "I planned to visit you first so that you might benefit twice. I planned to visit you on my way to Macedonia and to come back to you from Macedonia, and then to have you send me on my way to Judea" (2 Cor. 1:15b–16).

Now, Paul didn't cancel his trip. He was still going to visit Corinth—but he was only going to stop there once instead of twice. It was only a change of plans, not a snub. How many times have you told someone you planned to do such-and-such, but were forced by circumstances to alter your schedule and adjust your itinerary? It happens all the time. Our plans are always subject to change without notice.

But Paul's enemies decided to use his change of plans as a means of sabotaging him and undermining his reputation. They spread rumors in the church. They turned a minor change of plans into a massive character flaw. They told others in the church, "You see what kind of man Paul is? He's undependable. He has no integrity. He says one thing and does another. He's a liar!"

Clearly, Paul's enemies were making far too much out of a simple change of plans—but that's what enemies do. They twist the truth and turn an innocent situation into something monstrous. What did Paul's opponents expect to accomplish by criticizing his change of plans? What was their goal? Simply this: They were sowing the seeds of distrust. They were saying,

"If you can't trust Paul's word about his plans and his schedule, then you can't trust the word Paul preaches. If Paul is a liar, then his message is a lie."

It was not merely Paul's reputation and integrity at stake. Rather, his enemies wanted to undermine the sufficiency of Christ, which is the very core of Paul's preaching. They sought to silence the good news that Jesus Christ is the only way to salvation. They despised his uncompromising and adamant insistence that it is—

- Christ alone;
- faith alone; and
- grace alone

that admits us into heaven. Paul's enemies *hated* that message! Notice what Paul wrote: "I planned to visit you on my way to Macedonia and to come back to you from Macedonia, and then to have you send me on my way to Judea. When I planned this, did I do it lightly? Or do I make my plans in a worldly manner so that in the same breath I say, 'Yes, yes' and 'No, no'?" (2 Cor. 1:16–17)

Paul takes a moment to explain that his change of plans didn't mean he was undecided and wishy-washy, nor that he was deceptive. He would never say "yes" and "no" in the same breath. When he makes his plans, he makes them decisively and with honest intentions.

Then, in the next verse, Paul goes for the jugular. He knows what his enemies, the false teachers in Corinth, are trying to do. He understands their strategy. Their attack on him is really an attack on the gospel: "But as surely as God is faithful, our message to you is not 'Yes' and 'No'" (2 Cor. 1:18).

There are people all around us who hate the gospel of Jesus Christ, who hate moral absolutes, who hate biblical morality. But have you ever noticed they never come out and say so?

You'll see them interviewed on talk shows or you'll read their writings in newspaper columns and magazine articles—and they will never come right out and say, "I hate Christianity! I hate Jesus Christ! I hate the Bible!" They know better than to attack Jesus and God's Word in a direct way.

So what do they attack? They attack believers. They say, "Those Christians are so narrow-minded and intolerant. They're bigots. They're out of the mainstream. They just want to control society. They just want to control everyone else's life."

Nothing has changed, has it? Two thousand years ago, the enemies of God attacked Him by targeting the apostle Paul. Today, they attack Him by targeting you and me.

Unfortunately, we are all too quick to take the bait. We get suckered by their accusations and attacks. They criticize us—and we feel personally attacked. We usually respond in one of two ways: Either we become defensive and we respond with a counterattack—or we slink off and hide and hope they don't come after us again. Either we overreact—or we are too cowardly to take a stand.

Notice Paul didn't spend a lot of time defending himself. He didn't get tricked into making himself the primary issue. We're not important. Jesus is. We're not the real object of satanic attack. The gospel message is. We are just the messengers. So let's not make ourselves out to be more important than we are.

It's not easy to suffer criticism, slander, and unfair attacks. It's not easy to be called names like "bigot," simply because we say Jesus is the only way to salvation. These days, one of the worst things you can say about a person is "He's intolerant." If you want to be thought of as "tolerant" and "open-minded," you have to say "all roads lead to God" and "you have your truth and I have my truth, and we're both equally right."

Who wants to be called a "bigot"? Today, there is no social stigma to being an adulterer, a fornicator, a homosexual, or a pornography addict. You can practice any sin imaginable and be proud of it. Society will not judge you; in fact, society will make a celebrity of you.

But if you take a stand for Jesus Christ and biblical truth, you will be roundly condemned for being narrow-minded and intolerant. The only "sin" our society recognizes today is the "sin" of being "politically incorrect"—the "sin" of being a person of character, outspoken faith, and high moral standards. If you take Jesus at His Word and proclaim Him to be "the way and the truth and the life" and the only way to a relationship with God the Father (see John 14:6), you'll be hated and attacked by the culture around you.

When you are attacked, remember your opponents' ultimate goal is not to destroy you but to destroy the Christian gospel. It's not believers they're after; it's the truth of the gospel they want to destroy. So don't take it personally. Don't lash out at those who attack you. Instead, forgive them because they don't know what they're doing. Your real enemy is not made of flesh and blood; Satan is using these human beings as pawns in his war against our Lord and Master.

Claiming the Precious Deposit

The attacks Paul suffered from his opponents were painful, but he wasn't focused on his own comfort or on what other people thought of him. He was focused on God's interests, not his own. That's why Paul didn't spend a lot of time and energy defending himself against the accusations of his enemies.

Yes, he explained himself. Yes, he set the record straight and told the truth—but he didn't dwell on refuting every point his enemies raised against him. After explaining his reasons for changing his travel plans, Paul immediately went on to talk about Christ. That was Paul's focus—the message of Jesus Christ.

Paul said, in effect:

The things my enemies have said about me are untrue—
but let's move on to what's really important. In Jesus, all of
the promises of God have been fulfilled. In Jesus, all of the
blessings of God have been given. Salvation is only found
in Jesus. Joy and peace are only possible through Jesus. The
power and glory of this dying world are doomed to extinc-
tion. The power and glory of Jesus are eternal.

So heed the example of the apostle Paul. The next time
someone attacks you, let your response be: "All right, that's
your opinion. But I'm not here to defend myself. Instead, let
me tell you about Jesus. Let me tell you about His salvation. Let
me tell you about His forgiveness of sins. Let me tell you about
His love for you. Let me tell you about the gift of eternal life
He wants to give to you through His death on the cross. Let me
tell you about a Friend who will never fail you, never leave you
or forsake you, and never let you down. Let me tell you about
a Friend who longs to have a relationship with you. Let me tell
you He's the alpha and the omega, the beginning and the end,
and He's the same yesterday, today, and forever. Let me tell you
about Jesus."

You may ask, "How can I do that? How can I stand there and
talk about Jesus while people are attacking me, accusing me,
and lying about me? How can I focus on Christ when I am in
pain, in tears, in anguish over the things people are doing to
me and saying about me?"

The answer: You keep your focus on Christ the same way
Paul did when he was under attack. And how did he do it? By
claiming the precious deposit.

Paul continually practiced the second secret of positive living: He claimed the 100 percent deposit of salvation he received
through Jesus Christ. Regardless his circumstances, regardless
the obstacles and opposition he faced, Paul could always point
to that precious treasure. He was consumed with that deposit.

He continually lifted up Jesus, the One who paid the 100 percent deposit for his salvation.

You and I can live the same way Paul lived, claiming the 100 percent deposit of our salvation. When we claim that deposit, we become free of doubt. We are certain of the Buyer's intentions. We know He will make good on the deal. We know the day of closing is coming and we long for that day. We have no fear, no anxiety, because the deposit is already ours.

You may offer some of these excuses: "You don't know how cruel my mother can be." "You don't know how abusive my father can be." "You don't know my spouse." "You don't know what a monster my boss is." "You don't know how relentless and hurtful my enemy is." No, I don't know that particular person in your life—but I know Christ and I know the deposit He has given us, and I know it is sufficient for any afflictions we may face.

My friend, if you want to experience the power of positive living—not the limited and fleeting "power of positive thinking"—then claim that deposit as your own. It will lift you up 100 percent of the time, no matter who attacks you, no matter what opposes you. The deposit has been paid in full by Jesus Christ on the cross.

Anointed and Sealed

Paul goes on to set forth some profoundly reassuring principles regarding this deposit we have received:

> Now it is God who makes both us and you stand firm in Christ. He anointed us, set his seal of ownership on us, and put his Spirit in our hearts as a deposit, guaranteeing what is to come.

> *(2 Corinthians 1:21-22)*

Paul tells us God makes us "stand firm" in Christ. In other words, God has established us and set us on an immovable foundation in Christ. Moreover, Paul says God has anointed us and sealed us. He owns us, and He has placed His Spirit in our hearts as a 100 percent deposit—our guarantee of the salvation to come.

We hear that word "anointed" tossed around in churches today. I think many people have the idea an "anointing" involves something magical and mystical. Someone once came to me and said, "I heard about 'the anointing' on a religious TV show, and I want to know what 'the anointing' is all about and how I can get it."

Please understand: Every believer who comes to faith in Jesus Christ has received the anointing of the Holy Spirit. There is no such thing as a Christian who has not been anointed. That's why Paul tells us God "anointed us, set his seal of ownership on us, and put his Spirit in our hearts as a deposit."

The word "anointed" means *set apart*. A person who is anointed has been set apart for a purpose, commissioned for a ministry, and authorized to carry out a task. If you are in Jesus Christ, then you are an authorized ambassador of Jesus Christ. You have been commissioned by Him and authorized to act on His behalf. Your credentials have been handed to you by heaven itself.

Paul also says God sealed us as believers; He has "set his seal of ownership on us." In ancient times, kings had a stamp or signet ring, usually made of gold. When the king issued an important document, a small amount of melted candle wax would be dribbled near the bottom of the document. While the wax was still soft, the king would press the royal seal, the golden signet, into the wax. This would leave an impression in the wax, proof that this document bore the stamp of the king's approval and authority.

Paul is using this imagery to say to us, "We, as Christians, are stamped and imprinted by the King. We bear His seal. He declares His ownership of us and His approval of us for ever and ever."

When I was a new Christian, just eighteen years old, I was discipled by a man of great faith and spiritual maturity. This man was a simple launderer who ironed our family's clothes, and I loved and respected him. I gained many insights into the Christian life from this man as he mentored me in my early Christian walk. There was one aspect of this man's life that left him feeling dissatisfied and unhappy: he was illiterate, unable to read God's Word.

One day, this man prayed, "God, I want to read Your Word." Then he opened the Scriptures and began to read the Word of God. It was a miracle! If he opened a newspaper, he couldn't make head or tail of it. But if he opened a Bible, he could read. God supernaturally answered this man's prayer and gave him the ability to read His Word.

This man once said something to me that has resonated in my mind through the years. "Mr. Michael," he said, "let me tell you something. God does not write your name in His book of life with a pencil. When you sin, He does not get an eraser and rub your name out of His book. When you repent, He does not take a pencil and write your name back in His book again. Your name is not being erased, written, erased, written, every time you sin, then repent. That's not how God works. When you believed, He wrote your name in His book of life with the blood of Jesus Christ—and nobody can erase that!"

What a comforting truth. Our names are written in God's book for ever and ever with the blood shed upon the cross! The 100 percent deposit is the guarantee of our inheritance. It's paid in full—

And it's *nonrefundable!*

By remaining focused on this priceless deposit, Paul could view the actions of his enemies from a more exalted perspective.

Paul's attention was fixed on eternal things—matters of God's eternal kingdom and life in heaven with the Lord Jesus Christ. By contrast, Paul's small-minded opponents had nothing more important to occupy their thinking than Paul's travel itinerary. Paul could say to himself, "I have the good news of eternal life. I have received the 100 percent deposit of salvation—it's mine forever. If those false teachers want to make a big deal out of my travel plans, let them. In the eternal scheme of things, their opposition is just a petty annoyance, like a buzzing fly."

Just like the apostle Paul, you have problems to deal with, and those problems often loom large in your thoughts and emotions. You may have marital problems or rebellious children or troublesome in-laws. You may face bypass surgery or chemotherapy. You may be losing a business, a career, or a home. You may not have any problems at all right now—but tomorrow morning, you just might awaken to some calamity you never anticipated. Life is uncertain and filled with problems.

If you allow problem people and problem situations to get you down, it's because you've lost sight of the second secret for positive living—your priceless deposit. It's time to gain a new and exalted perspective on your problems. It's time to look at your suffering and affliction from God's eternal and heavenly perspective. There is no problem, no enemy, no tragedy, no affliction, worthy to be compared with your eternal future with Christ.

The priceless deposit is yours. Claim it—and see how your perspective on life is transformed.

Giving and Receiving Forgiveness

On April 18, 1942, Jacob "Jake" De-Shazer climbed aboard a B-25 bomber and took his position as bombardier. Minutes later, the bomber took off from the deck of the aircraft carrier *Hornet*. It was one of sixteen planes headed for Tokyo to deal a demoralizing blow to the Japanese mainland just four months after Japan's surprise attack on Pearl Harbor.

Jake DeShazer's plane traveled miles and miles of Pacific waters, crossed over the coast of Japan, and flew over the treetops to its target near Tokyo. Jake dropped his bomb load and blew up a group of oil storage tanks. Enemy flak shot holes in the B-25 as it flew on toward China. Hours later, as the plane was running out of fuel, Jake DeShazer and the other crewmen prepared to bail out.

Though Jake had been raised in a

2 Corinthians 2:5–17

Christian home, he never committed his life to Jesus Christ. He didn't believe in prayer. As he parachuted into the darkness, he didn't give God a second thought.

Yet, at that very moment, thousands of miles away, Jake's mother awoke and felt a great burden for her son. She didn't even know Jake was overseas, much less that he was jumping out of an airplane over enemy-occupied territory. She just knew she needed to pray for her son.

Jake DeShazer landed in a Chinese graveyard, fracturing several ribs. Hours later, he was captured by Japanese soldiers. The next day, he was brought before a military tribunal and the judge told him in English, "At sunrise tomorrow, I shall have the honor of personally cutting off your head." After a sleepless night, Jake was blindfolded and taken from his cell. He was led into the yard of the prison—but he was photographed instead of being executed. Fortunately for Jake, the judge had lied to him.

During the next four years, Jake DeShazer was kept in a small, dark cell. He was occasionally taken out to be tortured or interrogated. Sometimes he was hung by his hands for hours. Other times, he was strapped to a chair and beaten. He not only suffered from the brutality of the guards, but was afflicted with dysentery and other illnesses.

After two years in prison, Jake was allowed to have a Bible—but only for three weeks. At the end of that time, the Bible would be passed on to another prisoner. Jake read by the light of a tiny slit near the top of his cell, going straight through from Genesis to Revelation. As he read, he committed his life to Jesus—and he committed much of God's Word to memory.

One day, shortly after his conversion to Christ, Jake was entering his cell when one of the guards deliberately slammed the iron door on his foot. Seething with hatred for the guard, Jake seemed to hear the voice of Jesus say to him, "Love your enemies and pray for those who persecute you" (Matt. 5:44). The next day, Jake spoke to the guard in Japanese, giving the man a word of blessing, then asking him about his family. The guard was amazed Jake would repay his cruelty with kindness. The man responded by bringing Jake extra food and some pieces of candy.

In early August 1945, Jake awoke early in the morning with a sense that God wanted him to pray for a swift end to the war. He prayed intensely for seven hours straight—then he felt a sense of peace wash over him. He later learned that two atomic bombs had exploded over Japanese cities, forcing Japan to surrender.

With the end of the war, Jake realized God had given him a great love for the Japanese people—and that God was calling him to Japan as a missionary. After attending seminary, Jake took his bride, Florence, to Japan. Over the next thirty years, they led many people to Christ—including Mitsuo Fuchida, the Japanese pilot who led the initial bombing raid at Pearl Harbor on December 7, 1941. Fuchida became a Christian missionary and evangelist who toured the world, preaching before huge crowds.[1]

Thousands of people heard and responded to the message of salvation because Jake DeShazer made a decision to forgive his enemies and to bless those who persecuted him. That is the power of Christlike forgiveness.

God's Forgiveness Compels Us

In all my years in ministry, I have never met anybody who did not understand that forgiveness is a central tenet of the Christian faith. I've never met anyone who said to me, "Forgiveness? What's that? What does forgiveness have to do with Christ and Christianity?" To be a Christian is to be forgiven.

To live as a Christian is to forgive others. Anyone who is acquainted with the Christian faith understands the centrality of
forgiveness.

Though people understand that forgiveness is inseparable
from Christianity, many believers struggle with the reality of
forgiveness in their own lives. Many say, "I know God forgave
my sins when I committed my life to Christ—but I'm having
a hard time accepting this. I don't *feel* forgiven!" Others say,
"I know I'm supposed to forgive others as Jesus has forgiven
me—but I can't seem to let go of my anger and bitterness!"

Many New Age gurus and secular self-help teachers talk
about forgiveness. You often hear them say, "Forgiveness is
good for the soul." Or, "Forgiveness is good for your health!"
They appeal to our self-interest. They promote forgiveness as
just another self-improvement technique, but forgiveness is not
a vitamin supplement you can buy in a bottle and take once a
day with your morning orange juice.

Authentic forgiveness is only truly possible for Christians.
If you are not a follower of Christ, forgiveness makes no sense.
We can only know our sins are forgiven if we know God has
forgiven us—and we can only know God's forgiveness if we
have accepted the death of the crucified Christ as payment for
our sins.

Moreover, our motivation to forgive others is rooted in the
fact that God, through Christ, has forgiven us. The apostle Paul
put it this way: "Be kind and compassionate to one another,
forgiving each other, just as in Christ God forgave you" (Eph.
4:32). And Jesus Himself taught us to pray, "Forgive us our
debts, as we also have forgiven our debtors" (Matt. 6:12). The
Bible tells us God's forgiveness of our sin compels us to forgive
those who sin against us. Those whom God has forgiven have
no option but to forgive every repentant person who comes
seeking forgiveness.

Here we find the third secret of positive living: learning

to enjoy forgiveness. We will be able to live effective, joyful, positive lives when we learn to enjoy God's forgiveness toward us—and when we learn to allow His forgiveness to flow to the lives of others. Here, Paul personally demonstrates how the life-changing principle of forgiveness works:

> If anyone has caused grief, he has not so much grieved me as he has grieved all of you, to some extent—not to put it too severely. The punishment inflicted on him by the majority is sufficient for him. Now instead, you ought to forgive and comfort him, so that he will not be overwhelmed by excessive sorrow. I urge you, therefore, to reaffirm your love for him. The reason I wrote you was to see if you would stand the test and be obedient in everything. If you forgive anyone, I also forgive him. And what I have forgiven—if there was anything to forgive—I have forgiven in the sight of Christ for your sake, in order that Satan might not outwit us. For we are not unaware of his schemes.
>
> *(2 Corinthians 2:5-11)*

In just a few verses, Paul gives us seven vitally important reasons why we should forgive one another. Then he goes on to give us what I consider the most exciting visual image in the entire Bible—an image of how we can practice authentic Christian forgiveness. First let's look at the seven reasons to forgive that Paul lists for us:

Reason Number 1: Forgiveness Empowers Us to Defeat Pride

Why do we so often refuse to forgive others? Why do we withhold and postpone forgiveness? Because of our pride. Pride causes us to nurse grudges and nourish anger. Pride makes us feel entitled to our bitterness and self-pity. Pride drives us to retaliate.

"I refuse to strike back," Paul says in effect. "I refuse to give in to hate, bitterness, and revenge, all of which are rooted in selfishness and pride." That is what Paul was saying to the Corinthians when he wrote: "If anyone has caused grief, he has not so much grieved me as he has grieved all of you, to some extent—not to put it too severely. . . . If you forgive anyone, I also forgive him" (2 Cor. 2:5,10a).

What is the problem Paul addresses here? Apparently, one of the members of the church in Corinth had verbally attacked the apostle Paul. This church member may have spread ugly rumors about Paul, or perhaps he stood up in a meeting and publicly defamed the apostle. Clearly, this man's actions wounded Paul—but the apostle humbly shrugs off his own pain and says, in effect, "He grieved you more than he grieved me. Now he has repented. It's over. Forgive him and comfort him, tell him you accept him—and I will forgive him, too."

Here we see Paul's humility in action. He surrenders his own selfish right to feel hurt and offended. He thinks of the good of the Corinthian church—and of the man who attacked him. The forgiving spirit of Paul extinguishes his ego.

Now, there are apparently some people in the church at Corinth who are Paul's boosters, his groupies, his fan club. In 1 Corinthians 1:12, Paul referred to factions and splinter groups in the Corinthian church; some people say, "I follow Paul," others say, "I follow Apollos," and still others say, "I follow Cephas [Peter]." So Paul was concerned that the "Apostle Paul Fan Club" would want the offender to pay and pay and pay for what he did, even after having repented. Paul was afraid they might say, "No, Paul! Don't forgive him too quickly! He needs to eat more dirt first!"

So Paul says, "Don't punish the offender any more. I'm not bitter or angry. Don't worry about my ego. The man has repented and he should be forgiven."

Here, Paul exemplifies positive living. There is no room in positive living for grudges and strife. Resentment is negative; it weighs down the human spirit. Forgiveness is positive; it frees the human spirit to move out of the past and into the future. Bitterness steals our joy and destroys our effectiveness for God. Forgiveness delivers us, heals us, and empowers us for service to God and others.

Reason Number 2: Forgiveness Demonstrates Mercy

God was merciful to us in sending Jesus Christ as the sacrifice for our sins—and He did so while we were still in rebellion against Him. If God has shown mercy to us, we must show mercy to others. That's why Paul writes: "The punishment inflicted on him by the majority is sufficient for him. Now instead, you ought to forgive and comfort him, so that he will not be overwhelmed by excessive sorrow" (2 Cor. 2:6-7).

This man who attacked Paul was now suffering. The congregation punished him—probably through a process of church discipline. He responded by repenting. Now he was feeling terrible about his sins—and he was in need of mercy. So Paul told the Corinthians, in effect, "Don't punish him any further. Don't go after a pound of flesh. Be merciful. Show this man the same grace and mercy God has shown each of you."

Reason Number 3: Forgiveness Restores Joy

Paul tells the Corinthians that holding on to resentment produces excessive sorrow; therefore, forgiveness restores joy. Paul writes: "Now instead, you ought to forgive and comfort him, so that he will not be overwhelmed by excessive sorrow" (2 Cor. 2:7).

Forgiveness releases joy in the life of the one who is forgiven— and in the life of those who forgive. Don't let bitterness and resentment steal your joy. An unforgiving spirit will block your ability to pray freely and worship God fully—and it blocks God's answers to your prayers. Jesus said, "Therefore, if you are offering your gift at the altar and there remember that your brother has something against you, leave your gift there in front of the altar. First go and be reconciled to your brother; then come and offer your gift" (Matt. 5:23-24).

Those who have sinned need to seek forgiveness in order for their worship to be meaningful and effective. And those who withhold forgiveness need to make the matter right in order to have a right relationship with God. Our heavenly Father wants all His children to experience the joy that comes with forgiving and being forgiven.

Reason Number 4: Forgiveness Demonstrates Love

Unforgiveness is lack of love. An unloving person is an unforgiving person, but a person who loves is a person who forgives. It's that simple.

Without genuine love, a home can be torn apart; a friendship can be destroyed; a workplace can become unbearable; a church and its ministry can be shattered. So Paul said, in effect, "I refuse to live as an unloving, un-Christlike person. I choose to follow the example of my Lord and Savior. I choose to demonstrate love—even to those who have been unloving toward me." His words to the church in Corinth are words of love: "I urge you, therefore, to reaffirm your love for him" (2 Cor. 2:8).

Reason Number 5: Forgiveness Proves Our Obedience

When someone sins against us, we are actually being tested in the area of our obedience. God commands us to forgive the repentant person. If we withhold forgiveness, then we are disobeying a direct command from God. We are living in rebellion and disobedience. That's why Paul writes: "The reason I wrote you was to see if you would stand the test and be obedient in everything" (2 Cor. 2:9).

God commands us to forgive. Does God just want us to "forgive and forget" and never hold people accountable? Does God "wink" at sin? Absolutely not! Sin is a serious matter, and God is very much concerned with the way we, as human beings, treat one another.

When people sin, God desires they confess their sin and repent of it. If someone sins against you, God wants that person to deal with that sin and seek your forgiveness. But once the sin has been confessed and the sinner has repented, you must forgive—or you are placing yourself above God. You are setting yourself up as a judge over that person.

If you do not forgive the repentant sinner, you are acting in disobedience. You are failing the test. So Paul urges you to pass the test and demonstrate your obedience. Forgive those who sin against you just as God has forgiven you.

Reason Number 6: Forgiveness Maintains Our Unity

Throughout the Scriptures, in both the Old and New Testaments, we see that God promises blessings to believers who maintain a spirit of unity. The psalmist David said, "How good and pleasant it is when brothers live together in unity!" (Ps.133:1) And Jesus prayed to the Father, just hours before He went to the cross, that His followers might "be brought to complete unity to let the world know that you sent me and have loved them even as you have loved me" (John 17:23). And Paul wrote to the Christians in Rome, "May the God who gives endurance and encouragement give you a spirit of unity among yourselves as you follow Christ Jesus" (Rom. 15:5).

Here in 2 Corinthians, Paul again addresses the issue of

Christian unity, as it relates to forgiveness. He writes: "If you forgive anyone, I also forgive him. And what I have forgiven—if there was anything to forgive—I have forgiven in the sight of Christ for your sake" (2 Cor. 2:10).

Paul writes here of his own solidarity and unity with the Corinthian believers. Whatever they forgive, he forgives. And whomever he forgives, he forgives for the sake of the Corinthian believers. He wants to see the church in Corinth become strong and effective for Jesus Christ, and the only way this can happen is if all the Corinthians remain united by loving and forgiving one another.

There is nothing that destroys Christian unity faster than a spirit of unforgiveness. If you do not forgive your Christian brothers and sisters, you allow the body of Christ to be broken and dismembered. God cannot pour out His blessings on a divided and unforgiving church. If you maintain a spirit of unforgiveness toward your brothers and sisters in Christ, you *choose* to miss out on the blessings of God.

This same principle applies to the unity between a husband and wife. This is why Peter, in 1 Peter 3:1–7, talks about the need for mutual love, forgiveness, and submission in the marriage relationship. And he adds the warning: "so that nothing will hinder your prayers." Peter is telling us that if we pray for certain matters and God's answer seems delayed, it may be God is waiting for us to forgive one another, so the unity of the marriage relationship will be restored.

Reason Number 7: Forgiveness Thwarts the Schemes of Satan

Paul next speaks of the fact Satan seeks to destroy us and hinder our effectiveness for Christ. He writes: "in order that Satan might not outwit us. For we are not unaware of his schemes" (2

Cor. 2:11). Satan's plan for our lives is very different from God's plan for our lives.

God wants His children to be humble, joyful, merciful, loving, and obedient. Satan's agenda is for God's children to be cantankerous, angry, merciless, and rebellious. When you and I refuse to forgive, we are playing into Satan's hands. But we are not unaware of Satan's schemes. We're not fools and we're not going to let him have the victory over us.

Forgiveness blesses the one who forgives—and the one who receives forgiveness. Forgiveness blesses the home where forgiveness is practiced. Forgiveness blesses the church in which forgiveness flows freely. *And Satan does not want you to be blessed!*

Paul's Shout of Triumph

Paul then makes a sudden transition. Without even pausing to take a breath, Paul moves from a sermon on forgiveness to a shout of triumph. Now, there's no exclamation point in the original Greek to suggest a shout, but we can tell from Paul's words that his feelings are intense as he writes, "But thanks be to God, who always leads us in triumphal procession in Christ and through us spreads everywhere the fragrance of the knowledge of him. For we are to God the aroma of Christ among those who are being saved and those who are perishing" (2 Cor. 2:14–15).

To understand what Paul is saying to us, we need to grasp his imagery when he says God "leads us in triumphal procession in Christ." Paul is writing here of the Roman triumphal procession—a victory parade following a military conquest. Rome, in Paul's day, had built a vast empire through war and conquest. Whenever a Roman general went forth and conquered some region of the world, he would return to the city of Rome and receive the praise of the citizens in the form of a triumphal procession.

The procession would travel the main road through the city of Rome and pass before a reviewing stand where the Emperor sat upon his throne. There was always a certain order or pattern to these processions. First to pass the reviewing stand would be the government officials, the members of the Roman Senate. They were followed by the trumpeters. Next came people holding images and sculptures that symbolized the conquered land just annexed by the empire. Next came a white bull, which would be sacrificed to the Roman gods.

After this came the captives—the once-proud princes and generals of the defeated land, now marched in chains toward certain death. For these prisoners, this defeat was the worst tragedy of their lives, and they often wept, wailed, or cursed as they trudged along, forced by the lash to keep up with the rest of the procession. Following the captives came the spoils of war—treasures of gold, silver, ivory, and jewels piled on carts and paraded behind the prisoners who once owned them.

Next came the Roman lectors—teachers of the pagan religion—who carried the rods of their profession as they went. Next came the musicians. After the musicians came the pagan priests, swinging their censers filled with burning incense, filling the air with a fragrant aroma.

Finally, the most important part of the whole procession passed before the reviewing stand: the conquering hero, the Roman general. He stood in a gilded chariot pulled by four white horses. An ivory scepter was in his left hand and a laurel branch in his right. A slave stood behind him in the chariot, holding the golden crown of Jupiter over his head.

Following the general, his family passed by. His sons often rode horses, signifying their intention to one day enter the military and become conquering heroes like their father. After the hero's family came all the soldiers and officers who fought bravely and conquered the enemy.

As this procession wound its way through the city of Rome, crowds thronged on either side, throwing flowers and garlands. As the flowers were trampled by the soldiers, they gave off a sweet fragrance, which mingled with the scent of burning incense. The air was rich with that wonderful fragrance—the sweet smell of victory. The crowd would cheer and the soldiers would shout, "*Io triumphe! Io triumphe!* Hurrah for the triumph!" as this fragrance wafted over the crowd.

That is the symbolism Paul has in mind when he writes that God spreads "the fragrance of the knowledge of him" through our lives, because "we are to God the aroma of Christ among those who are being saved and those who are perishing." This is the grand and glorious victory parade Paul envisioned when he said, "Thanks be to God, who *always* leads us in triumphal procession in Christ!"

Note the word "always," because it is a very important word. Paul wants us to know that God's triumphal procession is continuous, it's eternal, it's unstoppable. Our victorious Lord Jesus Christ is marching in a victory parade, and behind Him are all of the faithful Christian soldiers who have battled Satan and sin.

Paul uses this imagery to convey a powerful spiritual truth: every moment of our lives, we are being led in a triumphal procession by our Commander in Chief.

We may not always feel triumphant. We may even feel the enemy is winning at times. But our Lord's victory is certain. Jesus conquered Satan, the enemy of our souls.

When you get up in the morning feeling tired and unmotivated, not wanting to face the day, tell yourself, "Today, I'm in a triumphal procession, marching behind my victorious General Jesus!" When you suffer hurts, losses, and crises that threaten to crush your spirit, tell yourself, "Today, I'm in a triumphal procession, marching behind my victorious General Jesus!" When difficult people, difficult problems, and difficult circumstances threaten to tip you into a black hole of depression, repeat the victory chant.

When Satan reminds you of old sins that God Himself has forgiven and forgotten, repeat the victory chant. When you have forgiven someone for a hurtful act, but old feelings of anger and resentment keep coming back, remind yourself again and again, "Today, I'm in a triumphal procession, marching behind my victorious General Jesus!"

The apostle Paul made another symbolic reference to the Roman triumphal procession when he wrote, "And having disarmed the powers and authorities, he made a public spectacle of them, triumphing over them by the cross" (Col. 2:15). Jesus has disarmed the enemy. Jesus has made us victorious over sin and Satan.

So whenever you face discouragement, fear, worry, anger, guilt, or any other negative emotion, stand shoulder to shoulder with the apostle Paul and shout, "Thanks be to God! Thanks be to the Conquering Hero who always leads us in triumphal procession! Thanks be to the One who spreads everywhere the fragrance of the knowledge of Jesus throughout all the circumstances of our lives!"

The Fragrance of Life, the Stench of Death

Let's take another look at the symbolic meaning Paul has embedded in the imagery of the triumphal procession. We must ask ourselves: What do the spoils of war symbolize? What do these wagonloads of precious treasure suggest? The precious spoils are the human souls you and I have helped to rescue from eternal darkness. These are the people with whom we've shared our faith and the example of our lives. They are the ones who have moved from death to life, from hell to heaven, because of our witness and influence.

And what about the sweet fragrance given off by the incense and the trampled flowers? The fragrance is a beautiful image of forgiveness. It has been said forgiveness is the perfume a flower gives off when it has been trampled underfoot—and that is exactly the image Paul suggests to our imaginations. When you forgive someone who has "trampled" you, your forgiveness is a beautiful, pleasing fragrance in the nostrils of God.

The perfume of forgiveness is also a pleasing fragrance in the nostrils of the people around you. It is attractive and enticing. When people see forgiveness taking place, or when they experience forgiveness in their own lives, they are attracted to the one who makes all forgiveness possible, Jesus Christ. When we forgive others, we show the world what God has done for us in forgiving our sin. We point the way to heaven, to eternity with God the Father, by grace through faith in the One who nailed all our sins to His cross. That's why Paul writes, "For we are to God the aroma of Christ among those who are being saved and those who are perishing."

Paul goes on to write to "those who are perishing," we are "the smell of death." But to those who are being saved, we are "the fragrance of life." Our lifestyle of Christlike love and forgiveness is like a sweet perfume to those who are being saved—but to those who are perishing, even our acts of forgiveness, our lifestyle of love, our Christian values, and our Christian gospel are like the stench of a rotting corpse. We who are saved are repulsive and offensive to the unsaved.

When I think about these words of Paul's and I think of the people I know who are rejecting Christ and the forgiveness He died to bring them, I weep. I truly and literally weep. Many times, as I have thought of those who have refused the forgiveness and salvation of our Lord Jesus, tears have rolled down my face. What is a sweet fragrance to us is the stench of death to them.

But whose death is it that fills their nostrils? Their own. They have refused again and again to trust Jesus as the only way to eternal life. Just as the conquered princes and generals marched in chains to their own deaths, unbelievers march in chains of their own making toward the death they have chosen.

Those who reject forgiveness from the hand of the Lord Jesus are destined for death. Those who do not humble themselves before Christ, who insist that all roads lead to heaven, who say they have no need of a Savior—such people are perishing before our eyes. They are destined for eternal death. To them, our presence is like the stench of death. They are marching of their own free will into eternal torment, and the fragrance of life, the fragrance of forgiveness, is to them an odor of corruption.

Those who have preached a false gospel and misled others to their doom are like the captive princes and leaders of conquered lands. In this life, they may have been praised for their wealth and power. They may have been "the beautiful people," the aristocracy, the intelligentsia, the crème de la crème—but God knows their hearts and their deeds. In God's nostrils, they reek of death because they are heading for eternal destruction—and they are dragging others with them.

As followers of Jesus Christ, we are in a vast triumphal procession, marching behind our victorious General Jesus. We have received forgiveness through Him, and we are to live our lives as channels of that forgiveness, spreading the love and forgiveness of Christ out to all the people around us. When we live as Christ taught us, forgiving and receiving forgiveness, we become the sweet fragrance of life to those who are being saved—and the convicting stench of death to those who are perishing.

A Procession without End

As you begin reading this passage in 2 Corinthians 2:5, it becomes clear Paul is deeply discouraged. He speaks of the grief caused by the hurtful actions of a member of the church in Corinth—a grief suffered by the entire congregation and by himself. His grief is compounded by the fact that some of the believers in Corinth refused to forgive the offender even after he had repented. Why is Paul discouraged? Because at this point in his letter, he is focused on the problem.

But at verse 14, we see a sudden and profound change come over Paul as he shouts, "But thanks be to God, who always leads us in triumphal procession in Christ!" What caused this surprising lift in the apostle's spirits? It came about when he focused on the *privilege* instead of the *problem*. The realization of the privilege of knowing Christ lifted Paul's spirit all the way to heaven.

It's a privilege to follow our General Jesus in this triumphal procession. It's the greatest privilege in the universe to be a part of His war of conquest against sin and Satan. And this triumphal procession has no end—it goes on and on forever. That is why Paul seems to shout, "Thanks be to God, who always—always, always, ALWAYS!—leads us in triumphal procession in Christ!"

And as we follow our General Jesus, we breathe in that beautiful, sweet fragrance of forgiveness. Through Him, we have received the gift of forgiveness and eternal life. Because of Him, we freely offer the good news of forgiveness and eternal life to the people around us, and we freely forgive those who have wounded us and sinned against us. As we follow the example of the One who prayed, "Father, forgive them," our lives become a pleasing fragrance before God and before the world.

A story is told of a priest in the Philippines. He was loved and admired by the people of his parish. He was such a kind, caring, compassionate man everyone who knew him thought of him as a saint.

But this beloved servant of God was burdened by a secret sin he committed many years earlier, while he was a young man in seminary. He had confessed that sin, repented of it, and asked God many times to remove his burden of guilt; yet he continued to be haunted by the memory of his sin. He had no peace. He felt unforgiven.

There was a woman in the priest's parish who claimed to have a gift of seeing visions. In these visions, she spoke face-to-face with the Lord Jesus. The priest was skeptical about this woman's claims, so he decided to test her. "The next time you have a vision and speak to the Lord Jesus," he said, "I'd like you to ask Him a question."

"What is the question?" she asked.

"Ask Him what sin I committed while I was in seminary."

A few days passed, and the woman came to visit the priest. "I had a vision last night," she said. "I spoke with the Lord in my dreams."

The priest felt a twinge of dread. What if Jesus had told this woman his awful secret? "Did you ask the question?"

"I asked Him," she replied.

"What did He say?"

"He said . . . 'I don't remember.' "

That is what the forgiveness of God is like. "Blessed is he," wrote David, "whose transgressions are forgiven, whose sins are covered" (Ps. 32:1). If we have received Jesus as our Lord and Savior, our sins are forgiven and forgotten by God. An endless experience of positive living is ours as we learn to give and receive God's amazing gift of forgiveness.

Overcoming Timidity

A number of years ago, one of the leaders in our church asked me a surprising question: "Michael, are you a shy person?"

I was amazed that he had picked up some clues about my personality few people ever guessed. I said, "No one has ever asked me that before. But the truth is—yes, I am a shy person by nature. In fact, when I was a boy I was so shy I couldn't look strangers in the eye. If a visitor knocked on our front door, I would always run into the back room."

When I tell people I'm naturally shy, they are amazed. They see me standing up in public, in front of a large audience and television cameras, speaking boldly—and even speaking loudly. How could God take a naturally shy person like young Michael Youssef and thrust

2 Corinthians 3:1–18

him into a very public ministry? To tell you the truth, I don't know.

I only know God arranged a series of circumstances in my early life—circumstances completely beyond my control—by which I was prodded and pushed far outside my comfort zone. God moved me against my will from a place of timidity to a place of outspoken boldness. I am not an outgoing, gregarious person by nature, but I have become intentionally and purposefully outgoing because that's the kind of ministry God has called me to.

I am continually aware of a sense of inadequacy. I am intensely conscious of my weaknesses, faults, frailties, and failures. I have often wondered, "Why would God take a person with my personality, my limitations, and push him into a very public ministry? Why wouldn't God choose someone with a naturally outgoing and bold personality?"

Given my druthers, I would much prefer to serve in the kitchen or the nursery rather than the pulpit. But God had other ideas. He took a shy boy, riddled with insecurities and inadequacy, and He gave that boy a platform and a commission to proclaim the message of eternal life. So as we come to 2 Corinthians 3, we hear Paul's great call to replace our natural timidity with a godly boldness. Here I feel a special sense of connection and identification with the apostle's message. I hear Paul speaking directly to me. I trust, as you read through this passage, you will hear him speaking to your heart as well.

Who Is Equal to the Task?

One week before my ordination to the ministry in 1975, the Anglican Archbishop of Sydney took me and all the other ordination candidates on a retreat in the country for a few days. He brought a prominent Bible teacher to lead us in devotions and a recommitment of our lives to the ministry. I will never forget the text this Bible teacher chose as the theme for our retreat: 2 Corinthians 2:16. At that point in the passage, Paul has just been talking about preaching the gospel of Jesus Christ and spreading the fragrance of the gospel to the people around us. Then he asks, "And who is equal to such a task?"

In other words, who is adequate and sufficient for the task of being one of God's witnesses to the human race? Who is adequate to the task of sharing the good news of Jesus Christ? The answer: no one.

Who is morally worthy of the challenge to warn people to escape the judgment coming on the world? And who is spiritually worthy of the honor of telling others of the blessings of salvation and eternal life? The answer: no one.

Reflecting on the words of the apostle Paul during the days of that retreat, I said to myself, "If the great apostle Paul felt inadequate to the task, then how much more inadequate am I? Paul saw the resurrected Christ on the road to Damascus. He was personally commissioned by the Lord Jesus Christ to take the gospel to the gentiles. Yet Paul said, 'And who is equal to such a task?' If this man had reason to feel inadequate, then it's all right for me to feel inadequate."

I think all of us, in one way or another, at one time or another, feel woefully inadequate about sharing Christ with others. In some sense, we all feel ill-equipped to tell other people Jesus and Jesus alone can rescue them from eternal judgment and torment. That's why God often has to:

- push us out of our cozy, cushy little nest
- nudge us out of our comfort zones
- prod us into accepting the honor and privilege of speaking to other people for Him
- place us in situations where we have no choice but to totally trust in Him alone.

We don't like to be challenged, uncomfortable, or placed in unfamiliar situations. We don't like to face situations that demand complete trust and dependence upon God alone. We like safety, security, and plush, cozy comfort. So God must often place us in situations that challenge us and stretch us, so we have no choice but to depend on Him alone.

A story is told of a king who had a beautiful daughter. Every young man in the kingdom wanted to marry the princess—but the king didn't think any of the young men were worthy of his precious daughter. So he designed a scheme to separate the courageous men of the kingdom from the unworthy boys. The king ordered a pool near the castle be filled with alligators—then he had all the young men of the kingdom gather around the pool.

"Whoever can swim across this pool," the king said, "will not only take my daughter's hand in marriage but will also receive half of my kingdom."

No sooner had the king said these words when there was a loud splash. The king looked—and saw a young man in the water, swimming and thrashing and kicking for all he was worth. Alligators closed in on him from every side, but he fought them with his fists and his feet. Finally, the young man came ashore on the other side of the pool, exhausted and bloodied but alive.

The king rushed to the young man and said, "You are the bravest young man in the kingdom! You have earned the hand of my daughter in marriage and half of my kingdom."

The breathless young man replied, "Well and good, Your Highness—but first I want to catch the guy who pushed me in that pool."

Sometimes for our own good and for God's own glory, He pushes us into the pool so we can learn to swim with alligators. And that brings us to the fourth secret of positive living: learning to overcome our natural timidity. We find this secret of positive living in 2 Corinthians 3:12, where Paul writes, "Therefore, since we have such a hope, we are very bold." Think about it: This very same apostle, just a few verses earlier, wrote, "And who is equal to such a task?" But now he writes, "We are very bold." In one breath, he said, "I'm inadequate and unworthy to be a minister of the gospel." In the next breath, he says, "I'm very bold."

What moved Paul from a place of inadequacy to a place of boldness, from a place of fear to a place of courage? In this passage, the apostle Paul gives us two steps for overcoming timidity and becoming the kind of bold witnesses for Christ He called us to be.

Step 1: We must rely totally on God and the power of His message.

Step 2: We must be willing to speak the *whole* truth.

Let's take a closer look at these two steps to overcoming timidity.

Step 1: Rely Totally on God and the Power of His Message

Overcoming timidity requires more than merely propping ourselves up every day with positive affirmations: "I can do it! I can do it! I can do it!" That's not positive *living*—that's positive *thinking*. The power of positive thinking may keep you afloat for a while—but it's temporary at best and can't be sustained. But positive living is permanent. It carries you through this life and on into eternity.

In 2 Corinthians 3:2, Paul said, "You yourselves are our letter, written on our hearts, known and read by everybody." Paul wrote many New Testament letters, and they are filled with powerful, life-changing truths. But Paul also wrote the gospel message onto the tablet of human lives. Empowered by the Holy Spirit of God, Paul preached, witnessed, made converts, and established churches. The believers whom he established in the faith became another form of epistle, written on human hearts, read by other people. Such "letters" of Paul, as the church in Corinth, became a powerful form of witness to the pagan culture of Paul's day.

Words that are merely spoken or written can be dead words that do not bring a dead human spirit to life. The most eloquent orator may mesmerize audiences with brilliant words, but mere words can never change human lives. But when the message of the gospel is inscribed upon our hearts and lives, God is able to reach the world in powerful new ways through His Spirit dwelling within us. Only the power of the Holy Spirit of God can:

- transform hearts and minds
- open blind spiritual eyes
- convict the human conscience
- turn Paul's words into arrows that penetrate the heart
- turn shy, timid people into bold, courageous ambassadors for God
- convert and save lost souls.

Because of Paul's confidence in the power and authenticity of the gospel message, Paul could live positively, courageously, and boldly. Because of the power of his message, Paul was unstoppable in the face of opposition, persecution, and misfortune. Because of the power of his message, Paul refused to focus on his own weakness or timidity, but on the Giver of all strength and confidence.

In verse 5 of 2 Cor. 3, Paul says, "Not that we are competent in ourselves to claim anything for ourselves, but our competence comes from God." Do you consider yourself a timid soul, hesitant to share the message of Christ with others? Do you wish you could make a difference in the world for Christ, but you hold back because you're afraid of what people might think of you? Then listen to what Paul is saying to you: The effectiveness of your witness is not dependent on your eloquence, your ability, your talent, your training, your title, or your position in the world. Your effectiveness for Christ does not lie in how well you plan or strategize, nor in how well you know your religious doctrines or keep a set of religious rules and ceremonies. There is only one source for your effectiveness for Christ: God Himself. "Our competence," Paul says, "comes from God."

Paul goes on to say in verse 6, "He has made us competent as ministers of a new covenant—not of the letter but of the Spirit; for the letter kills, but the Spirit gives life." Paul makes it clear God made us to be competent ministers of a *new* covenant—not the old covenant of the letter of the law, but the new covenant of the Spirit. No one was ever saved by trying to keep the commandments of the old covenant. You cannot keep God's commandments in your own strength. You can only keep His commandments by relying on the power of the Holy Spirit of God.

No one, no matter how disciplined they may be, can keep all the commandments all the time. If you break one, you are guilty of all. That's where forgiveness comes in, thanks be to God. Only through the power of God's Holy Spirit can you keep His commandments at all. So Paul tells us that, in order to overcome timidity, we have to be willing to live completely under the power of God and His message.

We live in a secular-minded society, and we have absorbed a secular mind-set. We think in worldly terms of abilities and limitations. We have ceased to think and act as children of the King of Kings. That's our problem as individual believers, and as the church of Jesus Christ today. Paul is saying to the Corinthians—and to us—we cannot overcome timidity unless we understand and rely upon the power of God.

As Paul told the Ephesians, the awesome, amazing power that raised Jesus from the dead is at work in us (see Ephesians

1:18–20). Recognizing and relying upon that power is the first step in overcoming timidity and living boldly for Christ.

Step 2: Be Willing to Speak the Whole Truth

To overcome timidity, you must be willing to speak the *whole* truth of God. Not a partial truth, not a portion of the truth, not a version of the truth, but the whole truth. Like everyone, timid people want to be liked. Many want to please others, so they tend to say what they think other people want to hear. They avoid saying anything that might make the other person unhappy or upset—so they often end up speaking only a half-truth or an altered version of the truth or sometimes no truth at all.

If you want to fully experience the power of positive living, you must stop wanting only to please people. You must stop distorting the truth in order to be liked. You have to risk being misunderstood, misconstrued, misinterpreted, rejected, and even hated. You have to accept the fact that some people will deliberately twist your words and slander you because they hate your gospel and your Lord.

In order to live positively for Christ, you have to come to a place where you can honestly say, "I will speak the truth, the whole truth, and nothing but the truth, so help me God!"

To be honest and fully truthful does *not* mean you must be spiteful, rude, obnoxious, arrogant, or egotistical. Look at Paul's example. He was dealing with a delicate matter here in the Corinthian church. His critics were going around saying Paul didn't believe in the Ten Commandments anymore. So Paul took time to proclaim the whole truth—and he did so without compromise, yet also without resorting to rudeness or an arrogant attitude or vindictive behavior.

Did that stop Paul's critics from lying about him and opposing him? No. Today, as in Paul's day, if you speak the truth of the gospel and you say that Jesus alone is the way to salvation, people will accuse you of arrogance and intolerance. They will try to browbeat you into compromising the truth of God's Word. They will try to silence you and render you ineffective. Above all, they will try to intimidate you into backing off your message.

Even people who aren't normally timid can sometimes be intimidated. A well-known television preacher was once asked on national television, "Do you believe that Jesus is the only way to salvation?" He fudged, hedged, ducked, weaved, and equivocated. He did not speak the truth as he knew it. Why? Because he wanted to be liked. He wanted to maintain his popularity.

How do I know that? Because a few days later he issued a letter of apology to his supporters and said, "I didn't speak the truth that I really believe because I was trying not to offend people."

Now, I'm not condemning this man. He didn't want to be criticized and condemned by the world, so he softened his stance and he watered down the truth of the gospel. I don't condemn him. But there's no getting around this fact: only a person who wants very badly to be liked would deny the truth of God's Word.

Paul faced the same kinds of pressures in his day we face in ours. The pagan world in which he lived was hostile to the gospel of Jesus Christ. The world of Paul's day didn't want to hear that Jesus was the only way to salvation. But Paul made up his mind that if it came down to a choice between being liked and being faithful to the truth, he would be faithful. So he jumped into the controversy of his day with his whole heart, and he spoke the truth of God's Word. . . .

And he let the chips fall where they may.

Paul spoke with tact. He spoke with a gentle and loving

spirit. But he spoke firmly and uncompromisingly. And he paid a price for speaking the truth.

Jesus and Jesus Alone

In August 2005, *Newsweek* magazine and the multifaith Internet forum Beliefnet.com conducted a survey of over a thousand Americans. The survey found that 68 percent of evangelicals (defined as people who call themselves "born-again Christians") believe there are other ways to God besides Jesus Christ. I was stunned and grieved to read this.

Soon after the survey results were announced, Beliefnet called me and asked if I would write a commentary on the subject for the Web site. So I wrote a piece called "Jesus Alone." Here is an excerpt from that commentary:

For some 2,000 years, people have used, abused, and shaped Jesus and Christianity to fit their personal and subjective construct.

Even in my own lifetime, I have heard Christ called "The Revolutionary Jesus," "The Marxist Jesus," "The Nazi Jesus," and "The Capitalist Jesus," to mention just a few.

I daresay that had this abuse of teaching been done to one of the founders of the other great world religions, the abusers might have been hacked to death in an attempt to avenge mischaracterization of the religion's fundamentals. Yet those of us who consider ourselves to be orthodox Christians do not respond this way—both because we believe in Jesus' injunction to His followers to turn the other cheek (see Matthew 5:39 and Luke 6:29) and because of our foundational belief in the sovereignty of God. Hence the statement attributed to Charles Spurgeon: "Defending the Bible is like defending a lion." The Bible speaks for and defends itself.

Nonetheless, from time to time, we are called upon to set

the record straight, drawing upon 2,000 years of Christianity that is centered upon the God who is the Alpha and the Omega, the one "who is, and who was, and who is to come, the Almighty" (Revelation 1:8, NIV). Today it is imperative that we as Christians point out the way in which society is altering the unalterable. We must defend the notion that God has not changed. . . .

We must return to Scripture, which clearly indicates that salvation does not exist apart from Christ and that we can be saved only by grace and not by works.

These aren't my concepts—they're from the Word of God. Jesus Himself said: "I am the way and the truth and the life. No one comes to the Father except through me" (John 14:6, NIV). It doesn't get any clearer than that. . . .

While our society continues to evolve, we must remember that "Jesus Christ is the same yesterday and today and forever" (Hebrews 13:8). He does not change. He alone is the way to God the Father, to heaven, to salvation. And nothing we can do or dream up will ever change that.

After that commentary was posted on the Internet, I received numerous e-mails. One man, who said he was a Christian minister, wrote, "I can't believe you're a leader of the church and you say that Jesus is the only way to heaven!" I wanted to crawl into a corner and weep.

Again I am reminded of the question Paul asks: "And who is equal to such a task?" Certainly, the person who distorts or denies the truth of God's Word is not equal to it. The person who preaches half-truths and falsehoods is not equal to it. The person who cares more about being liked than he cares about the integrity of the gospel is not equal to it. If we wish to live positive lives, we must take a courageous stand for the unpopular truth that Jesus is the only way to the Father, and no one comes to the Father but by Him.

We cannot earn salvation through good works or by being "good people." We cannot earn our way to heaven by keeping the commandments. The commandments were never intended by God to save us from sin. The Pharisees misunderstood and misinterpreted the commandments; they taught the people that keeping hundreds and hundreds of legalistic rules and rites would enable them to see God—but the Pharisees couldn't have been more wrong.

God didn't give us the Old Testament commandments as a means of salvation. Nowhere do we find that observing the commandments brings us grace, mercy, or forgiveness. In fact, the commandments provided the basis for damnation, not salvation. That is why Paul tells us that "the letter kills, but the Spirit gives life." The letter of the Old Testament law condemns, but the grace and forgiveness of the Spirit gives us salvation and everlasting life.

Dull Minds, Veiled Hearts

Paul goes on to refer to an incident from Exodus 34, when Moses brought the Ten Commandments down from Mount Sinai. As Moses carried the stone tablets, with the commandments engraved in the stone, his face was radiant and shining because he had been with God. The light that shone from his face frightened the people of Israel, so when Moses gave the commandments of God to the people, he covered his face with a veil.

Paul finds a powerful spiritual symbol in that veil. He writes:

> Therefore, since we have such a hope, we are very bold. We are not like Moses, who would put a veil over his face to keep the Israelites from gazing at it while the radiance was fading away. But their minds were made dull, for to this day the same

veil remains when the old covenant is read. It has not been removed, because only in Christ is it taken away. Even to this day when Moses is read, a veil covers their hearts. But whenever anyone turns to the Lord, the veil is taken away.

(2 Corinthians 3:12-16)

Those who try to save themselves by keeping the commandments, Paul says, have minds that are dull and hearts that are veiled and darkened. That veil can only be taken away when Christ enters the heart. As long as a person insists on saving himself through his own efforts, a veil of darkness covers the heart. Such a person wears the veil of the old covenant. All of his religious efforts and acts of do-it-yourself righteousness are doomed to end in death and darkness.

Like the fading glory on the face of Moses, the old covenant was never meant to be permanent. The Ten Commandments were meant to reveal the holiness and righteousness of God— an absolute standard of moral perfection that is forever beyond our reach. We can only receive God's righteousness as a free gift. We can never earn it by our own effort.

You know, neither the mayor nor a city councilman nor a judge has come to my door and said, "Dr. Youssef, you have been a good law-abiding citizen this year. We have been so impressed with you that we are going to present you with a special reward." It has never happened.

Nor has a police officer ever stopped me on the road and said, "Dr. Youssef, I stopped you because I want to give you a commendation. I've been following you and watching your driving for the past half hour, and I want to give you a reward for always observing the speed limit, stopping at stop signs, and yielding the right of way to other motorists. You have been an exceptional driver, and here is a reward for you." It has never happened.

But one thing I know for sure: if I drive too fast through a school zone, or roll through a stop sign without coming to a complete stop, or drive the wrong way down a one-way street, there's a very good chance a police officer will pull me over and write out a very costly ticket for me. And I will have no defense, for I fully deserve that ticket and all the punishment and expense that go with it.

Why? Because the law is designed to punish, judge, and condemn those who break it. It is not designed to save. It was intended to bring us to the end of ourselves. It was intended to show us we cannot save ourselves by our own effort. No one can keep the law perfectly all the time. If we could save ourselves by keeping the law, then Jesus left heaven for nothing, died for nothing, was buried and then rose for nothing.

The Purpose of the Law

So why did God give us the Ten Commandments? Once we accept the fact that the law condemns us rather than saves us, the answer becomes obvious: God gave us the law to drive us to Christ. The commandments were not given to us to save us, but to force us to recognize that, in our own strength, we are helpless and hopeless. The law reminds us we are desperate for God and for His grace. Unless we receive mercy from God, we are doomed.

As long as you think you are good enough and righteous enough to meet God, you have no need of a Savior. As long as you think your good works and religious activity will get you to heaven, you have no need of a Savior. As long as you think you have no sin and that you do not break God's commandments, you have no need of a Savior. The law confronts us with our own lostness and desperation. It rubs our noses in our own sinfulness and helplessness. It makes us realize God's demand is absolute moral perfection, and even one lie, one adulterous thought, one moment of covetousness and envy, is sufficient to condemn us to hell.

The commandments create a crushing, devastating awareness of our need for salvation and forgiveness. Only when we feel the full weight of our hopelessness and sinfulness will we cry out to God, "Save me! I am a person of unclean lips and unclean thoughts! I am lost without You. I realize my prideful self-righteousness is nothing but filthy rags. In the name of Jesus, save me!"

The person who has never come to the end of himself, who has never seen his own wretchedness reflected in the mirror of the Ten Commandments, will never cry out to God for salvation. Worse yet, he will never hear the voice of God say, "Welcome! My Son has provided the grace you need, and it is sufficient to erase all your sins—past, present, and future."

Jesus, the Son of God, was the only One who ever kept all of the law perfectly all of the time. We could never do it, but He did. That is why He could offer Himself as a perfect, unblemished sacrifice on our behalf. That is why He could step out of the tomb, offering us His forgiveness, His grace, and His new life. That, my friend, is the truth, the whole truth, and nothing but the truth.

It would have been easy for Paul to keep his mouth shut, to avoid angering his opponents, to speak only a partial truth or no truth at all. He might well have said, "Why rock the boat? My opponents have their opinion and I have mine. Who's to say what's true? Only a fool believes in absolutes. All truth is relative."

But Paul refused to take the easy road. He chose to speak the truth, boldly and without compromise. He had reason to take the easy path. He himself said, "Who is equal to such a task?" He might well have said, "I shouldn't say these things. I've already been through stonings and beatings and all sorts of opposition. Do I really want to rile up those teachers in Corinth and go through this opposition all over again?"

Paul understood such thoughts come from human timidity, not Christlike boldness. He chose boldness. He chose to overcome and vanquish every vestige of timidity within himself. He understood the power to overcome timidity is founded on two pillars:

- the power of the message
- the truth of the message.

Now you and I face the same choice. Will we choose the easy path of silence or compromise? Will we excuse ourselves by saying, "Who is equal to such a task? Not I! I won't even try!" Or will we follow the example of Paul, the example of Jesus—and choose the rugged road of boldness?

I won't kid you—the world is arrayed against you. The culture you live in is hostile to the Christian message. All around you, people in the entertainment media, the news media, the education system, and even in some parts of the institutional church are saying, "The world has changed. The old ideas about God no longer apply. We need to change the way we look at God and spirituality. We need a God who is relevant to the Internet age. We need a God who is reshaped in our own image, a God who will respond to our wants and cater to our whims. We need a God who will do what we tell Him to do."

Now, you and I know you might as well try to level Mount Everest with a teaspoon as try to make God conform to our whims and wishes. But that is the mood of the culture in which we live. That is the ideology of our age—and it is foolishness! The mighty Creator of the Universe and Redeemer of our Souls can only be received in humility. But that will not stop the opinion leaders of our age from trying to reshape Him in their own images.

That is what you and I are up against as God calls us to be witnesses in this world. That is the arrogant spirit that challenges us and hates us and seeks to intimidate us and silence us. And that is why we must overcome our timidity and become people of bold courage.

Hugh Latimer was an English minister of the sixteenth century. On one occasion, he was preaching at Westminster Abbey and among those in the congregation was King Henry VIII. After Latimer finished preaching, the king was displeased. He sent word to Latimer, ordering him to preach again the following Sunday—and to apologize for offending the king.

The next Sunday, Hugh Latimer stood in the pulpit and said, "This morning, I have asked myself, 'Hugh Latimer, do you know before whom you shall speak today? To His Majesty, the King—he who has power to take away your life if you offend him! So take heed that you do not speak a word that may displease him!' But then I thought to myself, 'Hugh Latimer, do you know whose message you have been sent to preach? The message of the great and mighty God, Who knows all your ways and Who has the power to cast your soul into hell! So take care that you deliver His message faithfully!'"

Then Latimer boldly and unapologetically preached the Word of God to everyone present—including King Henry VIII. Over the years of Henry's reign, Latimer was twice imprisoned in the Tower of London. After the king's death, Latimer was tried for his teachings by Henry's daughter, Queen Mary I (also known as "Bloody Mary"). In October 1555, he was burned at the stake on the grounds of Oxford University. He was executed back to back with another martyr, Nicholas Ridley, and as the flames rose up around them, Latimer shouted to Ridley, "Be of good comfort, Master Ridley, and play the man! We shall this day light such a candle in England, by God's grace, as I trust shall never be put out!"

That is true boldness. That is positive living. May God give you and me the grace to boldly shed the light of God's love and God's truth wherever we may be.

The Real *Fountain of Youth*

The Fountain of Youth is nothing but a legend—or is it?

2 Corinthians 4:1–18

The Spanish explorer Juan Ponce de León certainly believed the legend was true. He came to the New World as a member of the second expedition of Christopher Columbus. He conquered the island of Puerto Rico and became its first governor. During his time as governor, some of the natives of the island told him about a miraculous fountain flowing with healing waters. Anyone who drank from the fountain, they said, became young again and would never die.

This was probably not the first time de León had heard about the Fountain of Youth. The myth of the fountain actually goes back centuries before Ponce de León, to the third century. Three hundred years after Christ, a collection of stories called *The Alexander Romance*

told of the imaginary exploits of Alexander the Great. Though Alexander was a real historical figure, these stories were far-fetched and wildly imaginative—yet many readers believed there was at least a kernel of truth to them. In one of the sto-ries, Alexander and a servant make a daring journey through the Land of Darkness to find the springs of the Water of Life.

The Alexander Romance was widely read in Spain during the Age of the Explorers—and Ponce de León was undoubtedly familiar with the tale. So when the Puerto Rican natives told him about the Fountain of Youth, he probably thought, *Aha! A magical stream of healing waters—just like the stream Al-exander searched for in the* Romance*! The legend* must *be true!*

So de León went searching for the Fountain. In 1513, while he was sailing in search of the fountain, he discovered Florida. Coming ashore at the place now known as St. Augustine, he be-came one of the first Europeans to set foot on mainland Amer-ica. Ponce de León searched every river, lagoon, and swamp along the Florida coast, but he never found the Fountain of Youth.

I've been to St. Augustine and I've driven around the town looking for the Fountain of Youth, I've sampled the tap water from the city, and I can tell you the water there didn't seem to do me any good. I'm still getting older by the minute.

Some people will tell you the Fountain of Youth can still be found today—and they'll be happy to sell it to you. Of course, they'll sell it to you in the form of nutritional supplements, vi-tamins, diet pills, exercise equipment, hair restorers, beauty products, and on and on and on.

Look younger! Feel younger! You can look twenty again! You've heard these claims. You may have even bought some of these products. By now, you are probably convinced that there's no such thing as a Fountain of Youth.

But wait. Don't be so quick to dismiss the Fountain of Youth.

My friend, the Fountain of Youth is no myth—it is real. You can find it in the Bible—a fountain of miraculous, life-giving waters. It is available to you, and all you have to do is drink from it and you will have life, a wonderful life beyond your ability to imagine!

A Spring of Living Water

We see this Fountain of Youth in John 4, in an encounter our Lord Jesus had with a Samaritan woman. Jesus was sitting by a well near the town of Sychar, and a Samaritan woman came to the well. As she was drawing water from the well, Jesus asked her for a drink. Instead of giving water to Jesus, she gave Him an argument. But the Lord persisted and said, "If you knew [who I was], you would have asked [me] and [I] would have given you living water." (John 4:10)

The woman scoffed and wanted to know what Jesus meant by *living water.* So He replied, "Everyone who drinks this water [from the well] will be thirsty again, but whoever drinks the water I give him will never thirst. Indeed, the water I give him will become in him a spring of water welling up to eternal life." (John 4:13–14)

Now *that* is a Fountain of Youth!

Here again we see the distinction between positive *thinking* and positive *living.* Positive thinking is temporary at best. It requires a person to continually focus on self-affirmation and positive thoughts. Positive thinking must be continuously propped up.

But the positive living Jesus offered to the woman at the well is eternal. The one who drinks from the fountain of positive living—Jesus Himself—will never thirst. The life He brings us is not temporary; it is *eternal* life!

The power of positive living Jesus offers us is a power that springs up inside us. It will not insulate us from life's problems, but it will enable us to overcome life's problems. It will not shield us from the difficulties and challenges of life, but it will make us victorious over them.

As we come to the next portion of Paul's letter, we find Paul's fifth secret for positive living: discover and revel in the *real* Fountain of Youth, the living water Jesus brings. In this passage, Paul reveals two things we need to understand to drink from the real Fountain of Youth:

1. how to find the Fountain of Youth
2. how to appropriate and revel in its power.

How to Find the Fountain of Youth

Jesus told the woman at the well, in effect, "I am the Source of living water. I am the Fountain. You can't get this living water from any other source but Me. And I will give it to you whenever you ask for it." Paul also points us to Jesus as the only Source of light and life: "For we do not preach ourselves, but Jesus Christ as Lord, and ourselves as your servants for Jesus' sake. For God, who said, 'Let light shine out of darkness,' made his light shine in our hearts to give us the light of the knowledge of the glory of God in the face of Christ" (2 Cor. 4:5-6).

Where do we find the power of positive living? We find it "in the face of Christ." When you gaze at the face of Jesus, you recognize that in Jesus all of God is there. You understand that apart from Jesus no one can be saved.

As we gaze into the face of Jesus, something wonderful happens to us: our faces reflect the glory of His face. As Paul wrote in 2 Corinthians 3:18, "And we, who with unveiled faces all reflect the Lord's glory, are being transformed into his likeness with ever-increasing glory, which comes from the Lord, who is the Spirit."

Jesus and Jesus alone is the full manifestation of God, and

only when you look at the face of Jesus will you get all of God. When you gaze at the face of Jesus, He transforms you. His Spirit bubbles up within you. Your dead spirit is revived and transformed into a powerhouse. Your murky soul becomes a flowing spring of life. You move from despondency to optimism, from resignation to rejuvenation. You cannot stand still or remain the same. The real Fountain of Youth transforms us.

The Fountain also restores our strength and enables us to continue serving Christ even in the face of trials, affliction, and opposition. Paul writes, "Therefore, since through God's mercy we have this ministry, we do not lose heart" (2 Cor. 4:1). We don't go up and down, up and down, on a spiritual roller coaster. Our circumstances and our enemies may conspire against us and buffet us, but they cannot keep us down. The real Fountain of Youth, the living water Jesus brings, keeps restoring and renewing our strength.

Not only that, but Paul tells us the Fountain of Youth purifies our lives, our motives, our speech, our intentions, our hearts. He writes, "Rather, we have renounced secret and shameful ways; we do not use deception, nor do we distort the word of God. On the contrary, by setting forth the truth plainly we commend ourselves to every man's conscience in the sight of God" (2 Cor. 4:2).

When we drink of the Fountain of Youth, we receive a profound honor, a special privilege. Paul writes, "And even if our gospel is veiled, it is veiled to those who are perishing. The god of this age has blinded the minds of unbelievers, so that they cannot see the light of the gospel of the glory of Christ, who is the image of God" (2 Cor. 4:3-4). Unbelievers can't see the light because they are spiritually blind; those who are able to gaze into the face of Christ and see His glory have received a privilege beyond compare. They have truly seen the image of God.

There are many people who call themselves Christians today,

but not all of them have gazed upon the face of Christ. Not all of them have drunk of the real Fountain of Youth. They may belong to a Bible-believing church and they may know all the right doctrines and creeds. They may be able to use all the right Christian phrases and evangelical jargon. But if they have not gazed upon the face of Christ, if they have not received the real Fountain of Youth, if they do not acknowledge Jesus and Jesus alone as the full manifestation of God, their minds are blinded.

Everyone who has received the gift of living water that Jesus brings, that spring of water welling up to eternal life, *must* be willing to accept the conditions of that gift. Some people want to accept the gift on their own terms, in their own way. They want to be free to add to the gospel or subtract from it. They want to be free to improve on the gospel or modify it or accept a reasonable alternative to it.

Satan has deluded many people into that kind of thinking. He has whispered in people's ears, saying, "You can have the Fountain of Youth without accepting the conditions that go with the gift. You can call yourself a Christian while denying Jesus is who He claimed to be—the way, the truth, and the life. You can deny His deity, His lordship, His sufficiency, and His sacrifice. Believe what you like about Jesus, and if there's anything about Jesus you don't like or which makes you uncomfortable, leave it out, ignore it." That is what Paul means when he writes, "The god of this age has blinded the minds of unbelievers, so they cannot see the light of the gospel of the glory of Christ, who is the image of God."

You may say, "'The god of this age'? Is Paul claiming Satan is a god?" No—not in any real sense. But Satan is regarded as a god by the unbelievers. Knowingly or not, they worship him. They may worship Satan in the guise of some religious idol or deity. Or they may worship Satan in a more abstract sense, in the form of wealth, power, fame, sex, self, or ambition. Regardless what form Satan takes, people worship him because he has created a world system that panders to human whims and desires.

And Satan loves to lure people into the trap of being religious without being genuinely Christian. He continually tries to convince people they can have God's gift of the Fountain of Youth and salvation while living any way they want. That's the great satanic deception. That's the blindfold he's placed over the eyes of believers. They want to be saved while living their way, not God's way.

Paul goes on to say, "For we do not preach ourselves, but Jesus Christ as Lord, and ourselves as your servants for Jesus' sake. For God, who said, 'Let light shine out of darkness,' made his light shine in our hearts to give us the light of the knowledge of the glory of God in the face of Christ" (2 Cor. 4:5-6). You can't obtain the Fountain of Youth through good works or religious effort. You can't get it by working hard or giving everything you own to charity. Only God, the Creator of the Universe, can give it to you. Only the One who said, "Let there be light!" can shine the light of Jesus Christ in our hearts.

So accept the conditions God has set. Come to Him on His terms, not yours. Accept the free gift He is eager to give you. You will find the spiritual Fountain of Youth by gazing at the face of Jesus—that is, by recognizing that in Jesus and Jesus alone is all of God. That is the key to positive living.

Now let's look at the second question: how do we learn to appropriate the Fountain of Youth and revel in its power?

How to Revel in the Fountain of Youth

Paul next tells us about the power of the Fountain of Youth— and he uses the image of a jar made of clay to illustrate how we can appropriate and revel in the fountain's power. He writes, "But we have this treasure in jars of clay to show that this all-surpassing power is from God and not from us" (2 Cor. 4:7).

It is said "you can't judge a book by its cover"—yet people judge one another all the time, based on their physical appearance, their titles, their clothes, their net worth, their credit rating, the homes they live in, the cars they drive, the neighborhood they live in, the clubs they belong to, the school they graduated from, and on and on and on. These are false standards of judgment.

The homely, uneducated, poor man who lives in a decrepit inner-city tenement may have a heart full of Christlike love for the least and the lost around him. He might be one of the greatest in the Kingdom of Heaven. And the man who is highly regarded by everyone around him, who is on the cover of *Fortune* magazine, and who gives millions to worthy causes, including Christian causes, may be the least in the Kingdom—or he might not even be in the Kingdom at all.

God does not judge human lives by the "cover"—and neither should we. A book may be covered in shiny, 24K gold leaf, but the pages might contain nothing but worthless drivel. By the same token, a book's cover might be stained, age-worn, discolored, and completely unimpressive—yet, if you open it, you might find that it is a signed first-edition, a literary classic, a priceless collector's item.

That is what Paul is saying when he writes about having God's treasures in jars of clay. A clay jar could be covered in gold, yet filled with dust. Or a clay jar could be covered with dust, yet filled with gold. You cannot judge a treasure by the jar that hides it.

Note the historical context in which Paul writes this passage. The apostle has been under relentless attack and criticism. His enemies have criticized every move he's made, every word he's spoken. If they couldn't catch Paul doing something wrong, they would twist the things he did right and make them look wrong.

Paul called these enemies "false apostles." The false apostles invaded the church at Corinth and duped some shallow-thinking, undiscerning believers there. These false teachers and their dupes were constantly barraging Paul with accusations using half-truths, twisted truths, and out-and-out lies. If you've ever been the victim of a smear campaign or a whispering campaign, then you can identify with Paul.

But Paul's enemies discovered, much to their chagrin, that they couldn't destroy Paul's positive way of life. They couldn't dry up the real Fountain of Youth flowing within Paul, because it was not a superficial thing, like positive thinking. It was the very reality of Christ welling up within Paul. It was on the inside where nobody could touch it. Paul was living proof that the Fountain of Youth Jesus came to give us is something no one can ever take away; it refreshes us and cools us and strengthens us throughout our lives, and all the way to eternity.

When Paul's enemies found they couldn't undermine the Fountain of Youth within Paul, they resorted to attacking the container—Paul's jar of clay. There were no depths of evil to which these people would not sink. They even resorted to attacking Paul for his personal appearance and his manner of speech. As Paul writes of his opponents at a later point in this letter, "For some say, 'His letters are weighty and forceful, but in person he is unimpressive and his speaking amounts to nothing'" (2 Cor. 10:10).

Now, that's a low blow. Paul's enemies knew they couldn't beat him with logic and evidence, so they attacked him on superficialities. Perhaps they thought his eyes were too close together or his bald head too shiny. Perhaps they thought his voice was too deep or too high, too smooth or too raspy. We don't know the specific criticisms they made. We only know they resorted to cowardly and mean-spirited attacks.

Did Paul have human feelings like anyone else? Of course he did. But when you have the Fountain of Youth within you—the living water Christ brings—even the vicious attacks of your enemies don't get you down. You know you are involved in the eternal business of the Kingdom, and you have the Spirit of the Living God within you. You don't have to respond to every pathetic insult your enemies lob at you. In fact, your work for God is so important you simply can't be bothered with the superficial attacks of shallow-minded people.

When you know how to revel in the power of the Fountain of Youth within you, unfair criticism and foolish insults roll off you like water off a duck's back. People may lie about you and whisper about you and damage your reputation. So what? They are just attacking the clay pot. When you revel in the power of the Fountain of Youth, you know it's what's *inside* the clay pot that matters—and what's inside *you* is the power of the Lord Jesus Christ! That's the power of positive living.

Treasures in Jars of Clay

And remember, when Paul speaks of this power, he says, "But we have this treasure in jars of clay to show that this *all-surpassing power* is from God and not from us" (2 Cor. 4:7, emphasis added by author). Note that phrase: "all-surpassing power!" Paul reveled in God's all-surpassing power within him. He marveled at it. He rejoiced in it. He rolled around in it like a miser rolls around in his money. That power was the living water of Jesus Christ springing up within him, giving him the power of positive living—a power that made the most vicious and diabolical attacks of his enemies seem weak and foolish by comparison.

Paul didn't have to answer his enemies' charges. In fact, he didn't even argue with them. Instead, he agreed with them. He said, in effect, "What am I? Just a jar made of clay. You're right, I'm not attractive to look at. And I never claimed to be an eloquent speaker. I'm just a hollow container made out of clay. I'm worth nothing. Criticize me all you want. I really don't care.

Make fun of the container, if that pleases you. I admit my many limitations, weaknesses, and failings. But, oh, what a priceless treasure is hidden inside this unattractive jar of clay."

Years ago, a man criticized me and said some harsh things about me. I'm sure he expected me to put up an argument and possibly even fight with him. I listened to his list of complaints about me, and when he had gone all the way through this very long list, I said, "I hate to tell you this, you don't know the half of it. I'm far worse than you think I am."

He looked as if I had sucker punched him. His eyes bugged out and his mouth dropped open and he couldn't think of anything to say in response.

So I went on to say, "Sir, if you knew the real me, you wouldn't talk to me. You wouldn't give me the time of day. If I was on fire, you wouldn't spit on me to put the fire out."

Well, at that point, he seemed to be enjoying what I was telling him—just a little too much. So I added, "Now, don't you get uppity, my friend, because if I knew the real you, I wouldn't talk to you, either."

And that's the position Paul took toward his enemies: Let them slander him. Let them criticize him. What did he care? All they were attacking was a worthless jar of clay. The priceless treasure inside was all that was really important—and they could never attack that.

Paul didn't fear his enemies. In fact, I suspect on some level he actually pitied them because of their hard-hearted arrogance. When a person is full of himself, he has no room inside for God and His power. Paul's enemies had no room in their lives for the real Fountain of Youth. They rejected the gift Jesus died to give them. And those who reject and despise the gift of living water are to be pitied.

These are the shallow people to whom appearances, image, and style were everything. They focused on the externals instead of the internals and the eternals. They went thirsty because they refused the living water offered to them from the real Fountain of Youth.

Paul's analogy of storing treasures in jars of clay came from common practices of people in the first century. In those days, there were no banks, vaults, or safe-deposit boxes in which to store one's treasures. So the people of that era hid their valuables in clay jars. In fact, during my boyhood in the Middle East, many people still protected their gold, silver, or jewelry in that ancient way, by hiding them in clay pots.

Why did people use jars of clay to hide their treasures? These jars were perfect for that purpose because they were cheap and sturdy. They kept moisture out. You could bury a jar in the ground—and no one but you would know where it was buried. There is a legend in the Middle East of a man who buried his valuables in a clay jar—then marked the location by a cloud in the sky. When he returned to dig up his jar, he not only couldn't find the jar, he couldn't find the cloud.

Jars of clay were also used to store important documents such as wills, property deeds, and Scripture. You have undoubtedly heard of the Dead Sea Scrolls—roughly 850 documents discovered in eleven caves near the ruins of Khirbet Qumran, on the northwest shore of the Dead Sea. Many of those documents are texts from the Hebrew Bible, and they range from 1,900 to 2,100 years in age. They are remarkably well-preserved—because they were stored in clay jars.

So pots made of clay were used to store some of the most important treasures of the ancient world, from documents to precious jewels. But it's important to remember that jars of clay were also used for far less noble purposes. There was no difference between a pot that was used to hide a king's ransom in gold and a pot that was used every day as a chamber pot for human waste. A jar of clay can be put to honorable use or dishonorable use. It can hold desirable objects or distasteful objects. The pot has no intrinsic value. It's just a cheap, breakable, replaceable container. The only worth a clay pot has is the worth of its contents.

Focus on the Treasure, Not the Jar

Let me illustrate this truth another way: Put a basketball in my hands and what is it worth? About twenty dollars. Put that same ball in the hands of Michael Jordan in his prime and what is it worth? Millions! What makes the difference? It's the difference between Michael Youssef's hands and Michael Jordan's hands. The value is not in the ball but in the hands holding the ball.

In the same way, Paul is saying his value, your value, and my value cannot be found in the value of the clay pot. The value is in what the clay pot contains.

That is why Paul could say to his critics, "Criticize me to your hearts' content. I know my actual value is not based on the sound of my voice or my physical appearance. My true worth comes from what is inside me. My true worth comes from the One who owns me and holds me in His hand."

When the real Fountain of Youth, the living water of Jesus Christ, wells up in you and flows through you, your life has incredible worth and value. God uses frail, weak, inadequate people, mere jars of clay, to accomplish His will.

The power is not in the container but in what it contains. The power is not in *who* you are but in *whose* you are. The power is not in your title but in the title deed deposited within you. The power is not in your net worth but in the net worth of the One who owns you. The power is not in your gifts but in the Giver of the gifts. The power is not in what you can do, but in the One who can do all things through you.

Why do people become angry and defensive when they are criticized? Why do they feel hurt and resentful when their enemies oppose them and insult them? The answer is simple:

They have convinced themselves it's the jar of clay that's important, not the treasure inside the jar. They are focused on the outward container, not the living water, the Fountain of Youth within.

And there is yet another tragic consequence of focusing on the clay pot instead of the treasure inside: arrogance and pride. I have seen it happen many times over in my thirty-five years of ministry: A Christian, a servant of the Lord, gets a little success—and suddenly you can't talk to him. He now thinks he's a cut above everyone else. He's become a star and a celebrity in the evangelical Christian world. He has become vain and demanding, and now he lords it over the "little people."

How does this happen? How does someone go from being a servant of Christ to being a self-serving, self-important egotist? It happens because that person has confused the jar of clay with the treasure inside. Success has made the jar of clay think, *Oh, what a treasure am I!* And a jar that is full of itself is of no use to God.

Do you know what invariably happens to such people? Eventually, a crisis occurs. In their arrogance, they get involved in a scandal. Or there is a calamity or a tragedy in their lives. Or they simply reach a point where they discover the emptiness and meaninglessness of serving self instead of serving God. They tumble into the depths of depression and despondency because they are nothing but empty clay pots. They have either never received the real Fountain of Youth, the living water that comes from Jesus alone, or they don't know how to revel in its life-giving waters.

Continuously Renewed from Within

Paul understood the power of the Fountain of Youth working within him. He understood how to revel in it and appropriate its power for his own life. He not only reveled in it, but he continually drew upon it and refreshed himself in its living waters. Paul allowed the fountain within him to empower him to live positively amid negative times. Only through the power of the real Fountain of Youth could he withstand the opposition and attacks continually leveled against him by his enemies and by the painful circumstances of life. As Paul himself recalled:

> We are hard pressed on every side, but not crushed; perplexed, but not in despair; persecuted, but not abandoned; struck down, but not destroyed. We always carry around in our body the death of Jesus, so that the life of Jesus may also be revealed in our body. For we who are alive are always being given over to death for Jesus' sake, so that his life may be revealed in our mortal body. So then, death is at work in us, but life is at work in you.
>
> *(2 Corinthians 4:8–12)*

No one can stand being hard-pressed, perplexed, persecuted, and struck down—unless he is being continuously renewed from within by the power of the living water, the real Fountain of Youth. That was the secret of positive living in the life of the apostle Paul. He lived by the power of the Fountain of Youth that Jesus Himself caused to spring up within Paul's life.

You might say, "I've been a religious person. I've always gone to church. But I don't think I have received the gift of the real Fountain of Youth. I want a fountain of living water to flow in my life today." You can do that. You can ask Jesus to bring that into your life, and He will.

Or you might say, "I know I've received that fountain of living water, but I've never learned how to appropriate its power and revel in the joy it brings. When people criticize me—whether it's my parents, my spouse, my kids, my boss at work—I have always been hurt by it. I've been defensive and even destroyed by the criticism of others. I've been focused on the jar of clay when I should have been focused on the treasure inside. I don't want to live that way anymore. I want to revel in the fountain and let criticism roll off me, just as it rolled off Paul!"

My friend, today you can decide you will no longer listen to Satan's lies. You will no longer listen to the criticism of other people. Today, you can stand confidently alongside the apostle Paul and say, "Let people do and say what they want about this old jar of clay. I couldn't care less. The container doesn't matter. It's what's inside that counts—and I have invited the Lord Jesus Christ to come live within me, so His fountain of living water can well up in me. He's the treasure. I'm just the container. The treasure is all that matters—and the treasure is mine. No one can ever take that away."

True Health, Wealth, and Prosperity

From the 1960s sketch-comedy series *Laugh-In* through major film roles in the 1970s, '80s, and '90s, Goldie Hawn has had one of America's longest-running acting careers. Her father was a professional musician and a Presbyterian. Her mother was Jewish. Goldie was raised in a family that practiced the Jewish faith and also celebrated Christmas. So it was only natural that as an adult she would become . . .

A Buddhist.

Not long before writing these words, I came across an interview with Goldie Hawn posted at Beliefnet.com. The interview, conducted by Deborah Caldwell, was titled, "Goldie: Buddhist, Jew, Jesus Freak." The headline intrigued me. Had Goldie Hawn made a spiritual journey from Buddhism, then to Judaism, and ultimately

2 Corinthians 5:1–10

to Christianity? Or was she trying to practice all three faiths at the same time?

I read on—and my heart sank.

"What I've learned through my meditation," she said, "is a sense of equanimity, a sense of all things being equal. . . . The interesting part of my spiritual life is studying as much as you can. Islam and Buddhism and Hinduism and Shamanism and Judaism, Christianity—you try to learn what the precepts are, what the religion is, and ultimately, it's based in the same thought, it's based in the same outcome, you know."

What was her view of Jesus? If she was truly a "Jesus Freak" (her term) and if she integrated Christianity into her spiritual life, then who did she say Jesus was? A good and wise man, as the world claims? Or the Son of the Living God, as Jesus Himself claimed?

"He went to the desert," Miss Hawn said. "He sat quietly. He sat so quietly that he heard the voice of God. He heard the truth. He felt the truth. He was able to receive the truth because he emptied himself and he had the ability to do it. Perhaps that was his specialness, or part of it."

Miss Hawn has not looked closely at the life of Christ. Jesus didn't go out into the desert and hear the voice of God. He heard the temptation of Satan. And not once did Jesus ever say he heard the truth or felt the truth or received the truth. In John 14:6, He said, "I am . . . the truth." And He said, "No one comes to the Father except through me."

I'm reminded of that moment when Jesus asked His disciples, "Who do people say the Son of Man is?" They replied, "Some say John the Baptist; others say Elijah; and still others, Jeremiah or one of the prophets." And Jesus asked, "Who do *you* say I am?" And in a statement that explained the *true* specialness of Jesus, Simon Peter replied, "You are the Christ, the Son of the living God." And Jesus said, "Blessed are you, Simon son of Jonah, for this was not revealed to you by man, but by my Father in heaven" (see Matthew 16:13–17).

I feel an ache within my spirit as I think of how this talented, successful, intelligent woman, who speaks so highly of Christ, has nevertheless missed the essence of who He is and why He came. And my heart goes out to her because of what she said next—a tragic statement of belief that I'm sure is shared by millions of people who spend a lifetime seeking and meditating and making up their own religion:

"The view of yourself," she said, "is ever-changing because you're growing older, your body is changing, your face is changing, everything is changing—but you have a tendency . . . to grasp onto the ability to always look beautiful. . . . So if in fact I see an ugly picture of myself, which I've seen many times—it's like a stake in my heart. It's horrible—yet one day you're going to be very old and you're going to die and you're not going to look like this."[1]

In her respect for Jesus, Miss Hawn is so close to the truth—yet she tragically misses the solution to the very fear she speaks of: the fear of losing all the things that matter to you—youth, beauty, health, and life itself. It is the fear of aging, changing, and dying.

My friend, the loss of beauty and youth, the loss of our health, wealth, and prosperous way of living, does not have to terrorize us, like a stake through our hearts. In 2 Corinthians 5, Paul gives us his next secret of positive living: how to have *true* health, wealth, and prosperity that time and death can never take away.

Torn Between Life and Death

Paul opens 2 Corinthians 5 by comparing and contrasting our earthly dwelling place, our "tent," with our eternal dwelling place in heaven: "Now we know that if the earthly tent we live in is destroyed, we have a building from God, an eternal house in heaven, not built by human hands. Meanwhile we groan, longing to be clothed with our heavenly dwelling, because when we are clothed, we will not be found naked. For while we are in this tent, we groan and are burdened, because we do not wish to be unclothed but to be clothed with our heavenly dwelling, so that what is mortal may be swallowed up by life" (2 Cor. 5:1-4).

Paul is contrasting two opposite views of life. He contrasts an earthly tent versus a heavenly house, mortal life versus eternal life, being in the body versus being at home with the Lord, living by sight versus living by faith. One view is focused on the earthly, the mortal, the temporary, the things we can see. The other view is focused on the heavenly, the immortal, the eternal, the things we know by faith.

You would have to be from another planet not to know that the vast majority of human beings are focused on the earthly and temporary. Most people today are obsessed with acquiring and maintaining health, wealth, and prosperity in this life. People spend billions of dollars a year trying to hold on to their fleeting youth. They diet and exercise, consume vitamins and supplements, take injections in their faces, hire surgeons to liposuction here, lift there, and tuck somewhere else—all in a futile attempt to prolong their youth and the illusion of perpetual life.

We earthlings are obsessed with our investment portfolios and retirement accounts, with getting the absolute lowest mortgage payment possible, and on and on. No matter how much money we amass, it's never enough to feel secure. Even millionaires worry about waking up one day to find they have lost everything.

Don't get me wrong. It's not a sin to want to be healthy, fit, attractive, and prosperous. There's nothing wrong with wanting to be a prudent provider for your family.

But I'm here to tell you that if you think the health, wealth, and prosperity of this life constitute all there is to life, then you are in for a huge shock. If the sole focus of your time and effort is on acquiring greater health and more wealth in this life alone, you will miss out on the most exciting future there is. If you do not plan for the life to come, you are missing out on God's purpose for your life in the here and now.

The very reason the Son of God left heaven, was born of a virgin, died on a cross, was buried in a borrowed tomb, and rose on the third day was so you and every other human being on the planet might repent and surrender to Him and receive *real* health, wealth, and prosperity. Please understand I'm not using those three words merely as a metaphor to describe heaven. No, I'm talking about *true* health, wealth, and prosperity you can enjoy today, right now! Only when you take hold of that *real* life of health, wealth, and prosperity, will you be able to experience the life of positive living *in the here and now*.

We need to remind ourselves daily of this truth, because the whole world around us is trying to keep our minds focused on earthly things that are quickly passing away—physical beauty, physical health, money and possessions, status and pleasure. The world tries to keep our hearts bound to these perishable, temporary things, and that's why we must intentionally and continually remind ourselves of the imperishable, eternal treasures that are ours through Christ.

When our minds are focused on the eternal rather than the perishable, we will experience a life of positive living, regardless of circumstances, diseases, crises, enemies, and even the attacks of Satan himself. That was the secret of the apostle Paul's positive way of life. When he took hold of that secret, he was able to live positively in the midst of floggings, beatings, stonings, shipwrecks, illnesses, imprisonment, and attacks on his reputation.

Death threats could not intimidate him. Opposition could not stop him. The *real* life of health, wealth, and prosperity was such a tangible reality in his life that death—the ultimate terror to most people—was almost a friend to Paul. He was actually ambivalent about whether it is better to live or die—not because he was depressed about living, but because he was so excited about experiencing the life to come. That is why he wrote, "We are confident, I say, and would prefer to be away from the body and at home with the Lord" (2 Cor. 5:8).

Paul made much the same statement to the Christians in Philippi: "For to me, to live is Christ and to die is gain. . . . Yet what shall I choose? I do not know! I am torn between the two: I desire to depart and be with Christ, which is better by far; but it is more necessary for you that I remain in the body" (Phil. 1:21–24). Such ambivalence. To be torn between life and death. We shrink from thoughts of death—but Paul was eager to depart and spend eternity with his Lord!

Paul's mind was not on earthly things, such as holding on to his youth or extending his mortal life span or acquiring wealth and possessions. His mind was on the health, wealth, and prosperity that never fades—and his focus on the life to come is what made him such an effective servant of God in *this* life. The promise of an eternity with Christ was Paul's very reason for living, for getting up and going to work, for worshipping God and serving his Lord. And that must become the focus of our lives as well.

No Other Path

Goldie Hawn got it right in this respect: "One day," she said, "you're going to be very old and you're going to die and you're not going to look like this." The problem is she doesn't know what those who love Jesus will truly look like. She is speaking of the aging and corruption that takes place in our *earthly* bodies—but Jesus has promised us *resurrection* bodies, like the body He appeared in to the disciples after He stepped forth from the tomb.

The question is: Where will you spend your forever? Will you spend it experiencing the *real* life of health, wealth, and prosperity? Or will you spend it in a place of judgment and torment?

This life is passing away, and I would be lying to you if I didn't tell you there is a real heaven and a real hell. Jesus continually spoke of the reality of heaven and hell. He promised the crucified thief, "I tell you the truth, today you will be with me in paradise" (Luke 23:43). He told a parable that contrasted the fate of Lazarus and the fate of an ungodly rich man; the one was carried by angels to heaven while the other was tormented in hell (see Luke 16:19–23). Jesus warned of the day when His "sheep" would be separated from the "goats" based on how they responded to Him in this life (see Matthew 25:31–46). He warned that "a time is coming when all who are in their graves will hear [the Lord's] voice and come out—those who have done good will rise to live, and those who have done evil will rise to be condemned" (John 5:28–29).

The Son of God, who created the world, said there is a real heaven and a real hell, and we'd better wake up to it. That's why Jesus came from heaven—so whoever will believe in Him will live eternally with Him. It doesn't matter what color your skin is, how smart you are, how fat (or flat) your wallet may be. Whoever will believe in Him is assured of heaven. There is no "maybe" about this assurance. I *know*, without any doubt, the moment I close my eyes in death, I'll see Jesus face-to-face.

Some people will twist that around and say, "You believe you're going to heaven, but people who don't believe the same way you do are going to hell. Isn't that really an arrogant position to take? Isn't it more humble and tolerant to say there are many paths but one destination?"

I'm not speaking out of arrogance. I'm not saying that only those who believe as I do are saved. I'm only repeating what Jesus Himself said. He didn't say, "There are many paths but one destination." He said, "I am the way and the truth and the life. No one comes to the Father except through me." *Real* arrogance would be to say to Jesus, "Lord, You are wrong about being the only way. There are many paths, not just one. I'm sure You mean well when You say that, Jesus, but You simply don't know what You're talking about."

When I say Jesus is the only way to God the Father, I'm not saying, "Believe as I believe." I'm saying, "Believe Jesus. If you believe He was a great teacher, then how can you ignore and dismiss what He said? Believe Him when He tells you that He is the only way to God the Father. Trust Him when He tells you there is no other path."

From the Slums to the Mansion

In Philippians 1:23, Paul writes, "I am torn between the two: I desire to depart and be with Christ, which is better by far." Let me give that verse to you in the "Michael Youssef Loose Translation": "I enjoy serving God in this earthly life, but I just can't wait to experience that *real* life of health, wealth, and prosperity in the presence of Christ."

Paul's anticipation of the life to come enabled him to live above all of the trials and adversity of this life. His longing to see his Lord face-to-face gave him the victory over everything he suffered, from slander to violence to the threat of death itself—a level of suffering ten times greater than you and I will likely suffer in a lifetime.

So many people around us are terrified of death—but death does not scare a believer who has laid hold of the secrets of positive living. After all, what is death? It's our ticket out of the slums of this world and into the mansions of God. It's our transportation from disease to health. It's a chariot that takes us from the back alleys of squalor to the streets of gold. It's our release from prison to freedom. It's our passport from famine to feasting.

That's why Paul could stand confidently and taunt our last enemy with these words: "Where, O death, is your victory? Where, O death, is your sting?" (1 Cor. 15:55). Death is the great shadow of terror darkening the lives of the people around us—but death held no terrors for the apostle Paul. He sneered at death. He snapped his fingers at death. He showed us the attitude we as believers should have toward death.

I have to tell you honestly that before Jesus came into my life, I was terrified of death and judgment. There were times when worrying about death kept me awake at nights and troubled my soul in the daytime. But when Jesus came into my life and forgave my sins, I knew I passed from judgment to forgiveness, from death to life. The end of my mortal life ceased to frighten me. I knew death wasn't the end of my existence. It was merely the mode of transportation to take me to a new life with my Lord.

Someone once said that if believers knew what heaven with Jesus is like, they would jump off bridges and high-rise buildings to get there. I believe the apostle Paul would agree with that statement. To live is Christ; to die is gain.

It's Time to Think About Heaven

Paul writes, "Now we know that if the earthly tent we live in is destroyed, we have a building from God, an eternal house in heaven, not built by human hands" (2 Cor. 5:1). He is telling us that, for the believer, death is like being evicted from a tent—so we can go live in a palace.

We don't like being evicted. Even if we're living in a tent, we don't like someone saying, "Come on, get out, you've got to leave!" That's what death says to us: "Move on!" But Paul says to us, "So what if you must leave your tent? Look at where you get to live next. A mansion, a palace, an eternal house in heaven! Why complain about leaving your tent when a *palace* awaits you?"

Paul next contrasts our current bodies to our future glorified bodies. He writes, "Meanwhile we groan, longing to be clothed with our heavenly dwelling, because when we are clothed, we will not be found naked. For while we are in this tent, we groan and are burdened, because we do not wish to be unclothed but to be clothed with our heavenly dwelling, so that what is mortal may be swallowed up by life" (2 Cor. 5:2–4).

You're just camping out in that tentlike body of yours. It doesn't provide much shelter. While we're in the tent of this body, we groan and are burdened by illness, injury, sorrow, and loss.

I have to admit I don't like camping. God didn't make my body for sleeping on the ground, bundled up in a sleeping bag, my face and arms slathered with insect repellant. I went camping for the first time in my life in Australia in 1970, and it was the most miserable experience of my life. Call me a chocolate soldier, but the closest my body ever wants to get to camping again is a nice clean room at the Holiday Inn. That's just who I am.

You may be one of those people who loves to camp out among the trees and the bears and the mosquitoes. If that's your passion, you may be thinking, *What's wrong with living in a tent? A little roughing it is fun!* Yes, you might enjoy it for a week or two. But what happens to your tent after it has been out in the elements for a couple of weeks? The tent pegs start to come loose. The ropes sag. The tent material starts to wear. When it rains, water leaks in and makes a puddle under your sleeping bag.

So Paul uses a tent as a symbol of this earthly life. One day, my soul will leave this old tent and enter into a body that is truly a mansion, a luxurious dwelling—solid, secure, and eternal. Sin will not buffet that new body. Disease will not invade it. Fear can no longer make it tremble. Anxiety can't give a case of ulcers to that new body. Blemishes can't disfigure it, nor can pain torment it. Discouragement can't bring depression upon it. Sorrow can never rack that new body with sobs and tears.

As Paul told the Christians in Philippi, "But our citizenship is in heaven. And we eagerly await a Savior from there, the Lord Jesus Christ, who, by the power that enables him to bring everything under his control, will transform our lowly bodies so that they will be like his glorious body" (Phil. 3:20–21). That is the glorified body Jesus has prepared for everyone who believes in Him. It will be like the Lord's own resurrection body.

Now, when younger people hear old folks like me talk about heaven and the resurrection body, they often tune out. They think, *I don't need to listen to talk about heaven. Death is a long way off for me. I have plenty of time to think about death and the life after death.* In my years of ministry, I have buried children, teenagers, people in their twenties, thirties, and forties—young people in the prime of life. My friend, this life is uncertain. Don't put off thinking of heaven until some later date. Think about heaven now, wherever you are in life, whether you are six years old or 106.

When you know Jesus, death is nothing to be afraid of.

Long-distance or face-to-face?

Paul next says that death is nothing to fear because it is like moving from a long-distance relationship to a face-to-face relationship. He writes, "Now it is God who has made us for this very purpose and has given us the Spirit as a deposit, guaranteeing what is to come. Therefore we are always confident and know that as long as we are at home in the body we are away from the Lord. We live by faith, not by sight. We are confident, I say, and would prefer to be away from the body and at home with the Lord. So we make it our goal to please him, whether we are at home in the body or away from it" (2 Cor. 5:5–9).

If you've been in a long-distance romance, you know how hard such relationships can be. You are in one city and your loved one is in another. You long and pray for the day you can see your beloved's face and speak your heart in person instead of through letters, e-mails, and phone calls. Paul says that's what life is like for us right now. We're in a long-distance relationship with the Lord—but one day, through death, we will see Him face-to-face. What joy that will be!

Look again at verse 5: "Now it is God who has made us for this very purpose and has given us the Spirit as a deposit, guaranteeing what is to come." When believers receive their new glorified bodies, it will be the fulfillment of God's purpose for them. Now we have the Spirit as a deposit. Then we will receive the fullness of God's purpose for our lives. We will shed our corruptible "cheap suit" bodies that now clothe us and we'll be dressed in incorruptible "pure silk" resurrection bodies.

God's glorious purpose for us as believers is the ability to experience close, face-to-face fellowship with God. Does this thought fill you with excitement and anticipation? If it doesn't, then chances are you have never known the love and mercy of Jesus and the joy of knowing Him. You can do that now. You can ask Him to take control of your life and live through you, and your life will be transformed. He will bring you real health, wealth, and prosperity, and you'll finally know the power of positive living.

Here and now, in this present life, the Holy Spirit constantly confirms to us that we are God's possession. The Spirit witnesses with our spirit that we belong to Him. But a time is coming in a place called heaven when we will see the promise of the Spirit fulfilled—and we will see God face-to-face. In this life, the Holy Spirit gives us glimpses of what it's like to have fellowship with God. But in heaven, we will not merely see glimpses. The amazed eyes of our resurrection bodies will see the fullness of an intimate, face-to-face relationship with the Creator.

And that, my friend, is probably the most wonderful of all the fifteen secrets of positive living. Paul writes, "Therefore we are *always confident* and know that as long as we are at home in the body we are away from the Lord. We live by faith, not by sight. *We are confident*, I say, and would prefer to be away from the body and at home with the Lord" (2 Cor. 5:6–8, emphasis added by author).

Paul sometimes went through hell on earth, but he was *always confident*. Why? Because he didn't fear what anything or anyone could do to him. He knew that even if his enemies killed him, he won. He couldn't lose. If he was absent from the body, he would simply be at home with the Lord! So he could look adversity and adversaries square in the eye and say, "You don't scare me. You can't discourage me. So what if you kill me? I'm going to be more powerful than Superman!"

The attitude of Paul should be your attitude and mine. Do you have financial pressures? Laugh at them. You can look bankruptcy and ruin in the eye and say, "You don't scare me. You can't discourage me. I'm going to be richer than Bill Gates, Warren Buffett, and Prince Alwaleed Bin Talal Alsaud put together!"

You can stand up to sorrow and pain, cancer and old age, blindness and memory loss, and you can say, "You don't frighten me. You can't trouble me. I'm on my way home to heaven, to the mansion Jesus has prepared for me. Go ahead and torment this old tent as much as you like. You won't get within a million light-years of my mansion. Just wait until I get to heaven!"

How should a believer live in light of the glorious wonders that await us? You've heard it said that some Christians are so heavenly-minded they're no earthly good. Well, C. S. Lewis observed that it's the other way around—it's the heavenly-minded people who do the *most* good in this present world. In *Mere Christianity*, he wrote:

If you read history you will find that the Christians who did most for the present world were just those who thought most of the next. The Apostles themselves, who set on foot the conversion of the Roman Empire, the great men who built up the Middle Ages, the English Evangelicals who abolished the Slave Trade, all left their mark on Earth, precisely because their minds were occupied with Heaven. It is since Christians have largely ceased to think of the other world that they have become so ineffective in this. Aim at Heaven and you will get earth 'thrown in': aim at earth and you will get neither.[2]

If we wish to do anything of earthly good for our Lord, we must be heavenly-minded. We must be focused on the face-to-face relationship with Jesus that awaits us beyond this life.

The Judgment Seat of Christ

Paul writes next, "So we make it our goal to please him, whether we are at home in the body or away from it. For we must all appear before the judgment seat of Christ, that each one may receive what is due him for the things done while in the body, whether good or bad" (2 Cor. 5:9–10).

Notice that first phrase: "we make it our goal to please him." A better translation would be that "we make it our *ambition* to please Him." Perhaps the translators felt "ambition" has a negative connotation in today's culture. But there is nothing wrong with an ambition to please God. Ambition to do good is a good thing. There is selfish ambition (which is evil) and selfless ambition (which is good). Ambition to please God is always good, desirable, and holy.

"What motivates my ambition?" is the question we must ask ourselves. We should continually question and analyze our motives. A person who wants to be a corporate CEO should ask, "Why do I have this ambition to lead a company?" A person who wants to acquire wealth should ask, "Why do I want to make money? Is this a selfish ambition? Or will I use this money to glorify God and help other people?" The person who works long hours must ask, "Why do I work so hard? To please God? To please men? To please myself? Am I driven by love for God or by a sense of inadequacy?"

Is my ambition to please God—or to please myself? To glorify God—or to glorify myself? To accumulate treasure in heaven—or on earth? To seek rewards that perish—or eternal rewards? The reason we need to ask ourselves these questions becomes clear in the next verse: "For we must all appear before the judgment seat of Christ . . ."

What is that judgment seat of Christ? Will the Christian believers be judged to determine if they go to heaven or hell? No! A million times no! The question of heaven or hell, guilt or forgiveness, was settled the moment we trusted Jesus Christ as Lord and Savior. Our sins were paid for on the cross—100 percent, paid in full. So what is the judgment seat of Christ? For what are believers judged by Christ?

In the original Greek, the word for "judgment seat" is *"bema,"* which means *a high rostrum, an elevated throne.* Picture a set of stairs that go up, up, up to a place where there is a bench upon which Christ sits. When we arrive in heaven, we ascend those stairs so that (as Paul says) "each one may receive what is due him for the things done while in the body, whether good or bad."

The concept of the bema comes from the ancient Olympics. The judge of the games would sit on a rostrum—the bema—at the finish line and determine which runners came in first, second, and so forth, so that each runner could receive the reward he earned by running his race. At the heavenly bema, the judgment seat of Christ, believers will give an account of their lives to Christ and they will receive rewards according to how well they ran the race of life. These rewards are dependent not on the deeds we did, but on the attitude with which we did them: was our ambition to please the Lord—or to please the self?

Paul also refers to the bema judgment in his letter to the Romans, where he writes, "For we will all stand before God's judgment seat. . . . Each of us will give an account of himself to God" (Rom. 14:10, 12). No nonbelievers will be present at the bema—only believers.

Over the years, some have taught that at the judgment seat of Christ, all of our secret sins would be laid bare for everyone to see. This is not true. The Scriptures tell us our sins have been removed from us as far as the East is from the West. God remembers our sins no more. So if our sins have been obliterated from God's memory, they will certainly not be brought up before us again at the judgment seat of Christ. As Paul wrote, "Therefore, there is now no condemnation for those who are in Christ Jesus" (Rom. 8:1).

The sacrifice of Christ upon the cross has saved us from being judged for our sins. But we are still accountable to God for the way we live our lives. Because we are accountable, we will be rewarded. Paul said some of us will have rewards like gold and silver, while others—those who are saved but only serving themselves—have accumulated only the rewards of wood or straw. Put a match to wood or straw and what do you have? A lot of smoke and a charred smudge on the ground. But deeds of gold and silver will survive even the test of fire.

Rewards on Earth or Rewards in Heaven?

Let me tell you a true story. In 1946, twenty-five-year-old Akio Morita cofounded a company called Tokyo Telecommunications Engineering Corporation. Morita was a former officer of the defeated Japanese Navy and a trained physicist. He started his company with twenty employees in a bombed-out Tokyo department store.

In 1949, Morita's company developed the world's first magnetic recording tape; the following year, the company marketed the first tape recorder in Japan. In 1955, Morita's company produced the world's first pocket-sized transister radio.

The miniature radios caught the eye of the Bulova watch company, which ordered one hundred thousand radios—but with one condition: the company wanted to market them under the Bulova name. The Bulova deal was the biggest business offer Morita had ever seen. That one deal was worth more than all the assets his company possessed. But there was one thing wrong with the deal: the radios would say "Bulova" on them—not Morita's brand name.

Morita turned Bulova down. He wanted his company's name to become an internationally known brand, so Akio Morita said no to a fortune. When the stunned Bulova executives asked how he could turn down such a lucrative deal, he replied, "I am now taking the first step for the next fifty years of my company."

Morita later said this decision was the best of his career. His company went on to become one of the most successful in the world. The company later became famous for being the first to market VCRs and compact disc players. You've heard of Mr. Morita's company—though the original name, Tokyo Telecommunications Engineering Corporation, is probably not familiar to you. You see, in 1958, shortly after turning down the Bulova offer, Mr. Morita changed the name of the company to Sony.[3]

This principle is important in the business world—and in the spiritual realm. We are often called to choose between immediate meager rewards and future mega rewards. We live in a world of instant gratification, instant results, instant success, and instant recognition. Paul is warning us, in effect, "Be careful, lest when you get to the bema, you find you received all your rewards on earth and there are no rewards for you in heaven. Be careful, lest you cash in all your shares on this side of heaven and there are no rewards for you when you stand before Christ."

Throughout your life, you will face choices: Will I sin—or please God? Will I be selfish—or selfless? Will I be ambitious for my own ego—or ambitious for God? Will I accumulate treasure on earth—or in heaven? Whenever you face that choice, remember the bema. Remember you will one day give an account for the choice you are making today, right now, at this very moment.

Then choose wisely. Choose for eternity. Choose the rewards that never fade.

Mastering the Art of Peacemaking

The ancient city-state of Athens was home to Plato's Academy and has been called "the wellspring of Western civilization." In 431 B.C., Athens went to war against the city-state of Sparta—the Peloponnesian War. During the war, typhoid fever spread through Athens, decimating the Athenian Army and killing one-fourth of the civilian population. As a result, Sparta defeated Athens and pulled the city's walls down. Though Sparta was victorious, it was plague, not military might, that defeated Athens.

In A.D. 165, the Roman army returned to Rome from its conquest of the Middle East—and brought back a pandemic of smallpox. This plague became known as the Antonine Plague, because it killed the emperor himself, Marcus Aurelius Antoninus. The plague afflicted the Roman Empire for fifteen

2 Corinthians 5:11–21

years and exacted a death toll of at least 5 million. At the height of the plague, it was estimated that five thousand people a day were dying in the city of Rome.

The Plague of Justinian, which began in Egypt in A.D. 541, was the first known outbreak of the bubonic plague. By the time it reached Constantinople, it was killing ten thousand people per day and it reduced the population of the city by 40 percent. That plague killed about one-fourth of the population of the eastern Mediterranean region.

Eight centuries later, in 1348, bubonic plague returned to Europe, where it became known as The Black Death. The plague was carried from Asia by seafaring merchants and killed roughly 20 million Europeans—a quarter of the population—in just six years.

Again and again, plagues have afflicted the human race: A ten-year cholera pandemic from India to China, beginning in 1816. Another cholera outbreak in Europe and America in the 1830s. Another cholera outbreak in Russia in the 1850s, and yet another in America in the 1860s. And the horrors of plague have continued through the twentieth century in places like Indonesia, Bangladesh, India, Russia, and parts of Africa.

One of the worst plagues was the Spanish flu of 1918 to 1919, which was first identified among U.S. troops at Camp Funstan, Kansas, and which spread to almost every continent of the world, killing as many as 50 million people worldwide.

And plague is still a looming danger in the twenty-first century. On September 15, 2005, Brian Ross, of ABC News, reported that the Avian flu (H5N1 flu) could potentially kill as many as 1 billion people worldwide. At that time there was only one medicine that could treat the Avian flu—an antiviral drug called Tamiflu. It was manufactured by only one pharmaceutical company, Hoffmann-La Roche, Ltd., of Switzerland. The company could not keep up with worldwide demand. At the time of the report, the U.S. had only 2.5 million courses of treatment ready for use;

in reality, the country should have stockpiles of at least 20 million courses of treatment—and preferably 100 million.

As I think of the suffering and devastation all of these plagues have brought upon the human race, I can't help thinking of another, far more deadly plague. It destroys human lives, families, and even entire nations. It has afflicted every human being who has ever lived and ever will live. It is the plague that is described in the opening pages of the book of Genesis—a plague called "original sin."

This is the sin of Adam and Eve, into which you and I were born, and which we have inherited. Among the symptoms of this plague are: Wanting your own way all the time, not God's way. Cold enmity and resentment toward God for wanting us to obey Him. Resistance to the fact that He has provided only one antidote to the plague. Severe frustration when we refuse to accept the one and only cure. Eternal death, an endless experience of darkness and torment, resulting from the rejection of God's cure.

And now for the good news: There is enough medicine for all who want it. This medicine is available regardless of one's age, socioeconomic class, race, color, ethnicity, and country of origin. Moreover, this medicine is 100 percent effective, and all who receive it are instantly and eternally cured. Those who are cured experience deliverance, joy, and an overwhelming desire to recommend this medicine to everyone around them.

The cure deals with the root cause of all enmity and resentment toward God. It produces reconciliation with God. It produces forgiveness, relief from guilt, and unspeakable peace even in the midst of unbearable pain. It assures us of a bright future in eternity. It redeems us from both the temporal and eternal consequences of the disease. It delivers us not only from the symptoms but from the deeply rooted cause of the disease. It even provides permanent immunity against the disease.

When you receive this cure, you don't merely recover from

the plague, but you are totally transformed. You are changed from an enemy of God to a friend of God, from an alien to an adopted child of God, from estrangement to an intimate relationship with God, from sickness to health, from rebellion to devotion, from death to life.

All this is yours for the asking because Someone has paid the price to provide this medicine. And make no mistake about this: there can be no reconciliation unless someone pays the price.

Ambassadors for Christ

Take a relationship between a husband and a wife. When sin comes between a husband and a wife, estrangement and coldness set in. Suddenly, there is a state of alienation between two people whom God has united as one. To heal that division, these two people must reconcile—but there can be no reconciliation unless the guilty party or parties humble themselves, acknowledge their sin, and ask forgiveness. Someone must pay the price for reconciliation.

In the same way, God created us to be united with Him. But sin has come between us and God. There is estrangement, coldness, and alienation there. Because of original sin, we were born into a state of enmity with God. We cannot overcome this state of enmity with God unless Somebody pays the price.

Thank God that the second Person of the Trinity, Jesus Christ, voluntarily agreed to pay the price so that, by faith in Him, we could be reconciled to God the Father. The central deception of all the false religions of the world is that they teach that human beings can be reconciled to God without accepting the treatment prescribed by the Great Physician, the Lord Jesus Christ.

Some of these false religions depict their gods as angry, hostile, and vengeful. The rage of these gods must be appeased.

That's why so many pagan gods have such a bloodstained history. Other false religions have gods who appear apathetic and indifferent to human suffering, human need, and human cries for help.

But the very core of the Christian faith is that our God, the Creator of heaven and earth, is neither hostile nor indifferent. Our God is a loving Father who sent His only Son to be our Savior. God is continually reaching down to us in our helplessness and hopelessness. He cannot be appeased by anything we can do—our sacrifices, our good works, our self-abasement, our prayers, and our pleadings. But we don't have to appease Him. He has paid the price for us, and all we have to do—all we *can* do—is accept His free gift.

Our reconciliation with God required the death of His Son, and the Son willingly laid His life down for our sake. He died and rose again so we can live forever with Him. That's good news—yet there is even more good news: anyone who is reconciled with God, and has received the one and only cure from Him, *is now an ambassador for God!* What a privilege and honor God has given to you and me.

What is an ambassador? An ambassador is an authorized diplomatic messenger or representative, an instrument of reconciliation, an agent of peacemaking. As ambassadors of Christ, we point people to the only way they can be reconciled to God. We show people where they can find the only cure for the plague that is killing them. We point the way to peace with God.

Here we see the seventh of the fifteen secrets for positive living: mastering the art of peacemaking.

Our Colossal Failure

In ancient days, the greatest honor the king could give you as one of his subjects was to appoint you as his ambassador to another country. In those times, when an ambassador spoke, it was understood that the king had spoken. An ambassador did not act on his own behalf but on behalf of his king. The ambassador lived as a foreigner in a foreign land because all of his authority came from his king in his home country. The more powerful the king, the greater the responsibility the ambassador had.

I have seen this principle firsthand. In many of the countries I've visited, I've seen when an ambassador of a tiny country speaks, it doesn't carry the same weight as when the ambassador of the United States of America speaks. What makes the difference? It's not the personality of the ambassador. It's the power of the king and the country he represents.

My friend, one of our great mistakes as twenty-first-century followers of Christ is that we have failed to realize *we are ambassadors of the King of Kings!* It's time to wake up and recognize who God truly is—and who we are as His ambassadors. As the fully authorized ambassadors of the King of Kings, we represent:

- the power of our King
- the authority of our King
- the majesty of our King
- and the message of our King.

The King of Kings did not merely make us ambassadors, He authorized us to announce to the world His cure for the sin plague. He has sent us out into the world with His message of reconciliation with God and forgiveness by God. People all around us are desperate to hear the message of healing and forgiveness, redemption and restoration. They are desperate to hear the good news of Jesus Christ.

"I Am an Ambassador!"

In his 1936 short story "The Capital of the World," Ernest Hemingway mentions a folk story about a father who was looking for his runaway son. The father went to Madrid and placed a classified ad in the personal columns of the largest newspaper in the city. The ad read: "Paco, meet me at Hotel Montana, noon Tuesday. All is forgiven. Papa."

The following day, the newspaper came out. The Spanish Civil Guard had to be called out to disperse the crowd because more than eight hundred young men named Paco answered the ad.[1]

The human race is desperate for reconciliation with the Father, and longing for a word of forgiveness from Him. All of humanity seeks a cure for the plague that afflicts us.

Paul understood this universal desolation and desperation, and he had a deep passion to spread the good news to anyone who would listen. He would not allow the death threats, slander, and relentless opposition of his enemies to discourage him or dissuade him. Let the false teachers assault his integrity. Let his opponents call him a fool and a madman. He was an ambassador of the King of Kings, and he would not be deterred from carrying out his mission in God's name. He persevered in the power of positive living.

Paul rushes to focus on the unparalleled privilege God has given him as an ambassador for Christ—a privilege that every believer has received from the Father. He writes, "All this is from God, who reconciled us to himself through Christ and gave us the ministry of reconciliation: that God was reconciling the world to himself in Christ, not counting men's sins against them. And he has committed to us the message of reconciliation. We are therefore Christ's ambassadors, as though God were making his appeal through us. We implore you on Christ's behalf: Be reconciled to God.

God made him who had no sin to be sin for us, so that in him we might become the righteousness of God" (2 Cor. 5:18–21).

Does Paul say, "I am Christ's ambassador"? No. He says, "We are Christ's ambassadors." God did not redeem you and save you eternally only to reconcile you to Himself. God not only transformed us from enemies to inheritors of His wealth, He also called us as ambassadors, representing Himself and His kingdom before this fallen world.

So from now on, when somebody asks you what you do for a living, don't answer, "A real estate broker" or "A teacher" or "A plumber" or "A lawyer." Instead, say, "I am an ambassador." I've tried this a few times myself. The problem with me is that people look at me and they say, "Oh? Of what country?"

If anyone asks you, "Whom do you represent? What country do you speak for as ambassador?" you can simply say: "I speak for the King of Glory. I act on behalf of the King of Kings and Lord of Lords. I have the King's authority to proclaim the message of reconciliation to God."

Here is something I often try to do: No matter how heavy my burden, how difficult my circumstances may be, how hard my lot in life is, how severe my challenges and unbearable my pain—I just start living and acting as an ambassador of the Lord of Glory and I soon find my burdens become as light as a feather. Start sharing the good news with others and showing fearful, guilt-ridden people that Jesus saves and delivers—and I promise you will have a completely different perspective on your worries and afflictions.

As a representative of the King of Kings, you have a wonderful message for the world: "The war is over! Peace is declared between God and humanity! All is forgiven! Come through His Son Jesus and be reconciled to the Father!" You are His messenger, His spokesman. You are doing His will, serving His purpose, and conducting His business. When you see yourself in that light, there is nothing that can stop you, there is no one who can get you down for long.

I know you face discouragements and challenges. I do, too. Satan uses affliction in my life to trip me up and hinder my effectiveness for God. But when I remind myself of the authority I have and the privilege I have as an ambassador of the King, I can't stay down for long. I get up in a hurry and jump right back into the fray.

"We are therefore Christ's ambassadors," wrote Paul, "as though God were making his appeal through us. We implore you on Christ's behalf: Be reconciled to God." That is our identity. That is our message. What an honor and a privilege our Lord has given us.

"What If . . . ?"

Martin Niemöller was a German pastor in the Evangelical Lutheran Church during World War II. As a cofounder of the anti-Nazi Confessing Church, Niemöller courageously opposed the Nazis until his arrest by the Gestapo in 1937. He was imprisoned in Sachsenhausen and Dachau concentration camps for eight years and narrowly escaped execution.

Shortly before his death in 1984 at age 92, Niemöller told a few friends of a strange recurring dream. In this dream, Niemöller witnessed the great day of God's judgment of humanity, when everyone came before the Lord Jesus to be judged. To his surprise, Niemöller saw Adolf Hitler standing before Jesus. The Lord had one arm compassionately around Hitler and He said, "Why, Adolf, why? What drove you to kill so many? Why were you so cruel?"

And Hitler wept and hung his head, sobbing, "I didn't know about You! No one ever told me how much You love me!"

At this point, Niemöller would awaken in a cold sweat, consumed with guilt. Why did he feel guilty? Because, in the

1930s, before the war began, Niemöller had a number of face-to-face meetings with Adolf Hitler. As a leader of the Evangelical Lutheran Church, Niemöller spoke personally with Hitler, not just once but many times. In all of those meetings, Martin Niemöller never once spoke as an ambassador of Jesus Christ, bringing a message of reconciliation from the Father. Never once had he said, "God loves you, Herr Hitler. He loves you so much He sent His Son to die for you. The war between you and God is over. All will be forgiven if you simply accept this gift. You can have peace with God through His Son."

Martin Niemöller couldn't help wondering how history might have turned out differently—had he come to Hitler, not as a leader of the Lutheran Church, but as an ambassador of the King of Glory. How might the world have changed—had Niemöller mastered the art of peacemaking in his conversations with the Nazi dictator? He would never know—and he was haunted by that sense of "What if . . . ?"

There are people all around you who have never heard the good news that the war is over, that peace with God is at hand. They have never heard that all will be forgiven if they simply accept the gift of salvation Jesus offers them, paid in full. They are waiting for a message of hope from a peacemaker, an ambassador of the King of Glory.

You are that ambassador. Don't delay. Don't neglect the honor God has given you. Find a hurt and heal it. Find a need and meet it. Find someone who is lost and point the way to peace.

We are Christ's ambassadors, and we implore everyone around us on His behalf: "Be reconciled to God." That is the cure for the sin plague. That is the pathway to positive living.

The Power of Example

Pat Williams is the cofounder and vice president of the Orlando Magic NBA franchise, and the author of such books as *Coaching Your Kids to Be Leaders* and *The Paradox of Power*. He tells the story of his early years.

2 Corinthians 6:1–7:1

"I have an exciting life as a leader in professional sports," Pat said, "and I owe it all to my parents, Jim and Ellen Williams. From my earliest years, they prepared me for the life I lead today.

"Dad gave me my first baseball glove when I was three years old and took me to my first big-league game when I was seven. It was a doubleheader at Shibe Park, the Philadelphia Athletics hosting the Cleveland Indians. What an experience! I yelled my head off, gobbled up hot dogs and washed them down with soda pop. I had the time

of my life. Before the day was over, I knew I wanted to spend my life in professional sports.

"Mom and Dad were baseball fans. If I wasn't playing catch with Dad, then Mom would fill in. We set up a makeshift pitcher's mound and home plate in the backyard, and I would practice pitching and batting with my parents. One time when I was seven, Mom was in her batting stance at the plate and I pitched her my fastball. She swung—and lined the ball straight back at me, hitting me in the eye. I dropped like a bag of wet sand, out cold. Mom thought she'd killed me, but I came to and had the most gorgeous black eye you ever saw.

"I always saw my father as a calm, easygoing man who worked hard to provide for his family. As a disciplinarian, he was loving but firm. He kept a paint paddle hanging on the kitchen wall—he called it his 'Patrick Persuader.' Believe me, I didn't need to be 'persuaded' very often.

"Dad was a teacher and coach at a private school, and my earliest memories involve being with my dad in the locker room or on the sidelines. I watched him coach the team, I saw how he instructed and motivated his players, and I soaked up his values. I think a lot of my own leadership ability was absorbed by osmosis, just watching Dad's example. He often used my passion for sports to teach me life lessons about perseverance, fairness, integrity, courage, and endurance.

"I think of myself as Jim Williams' protegé. I am who I am because he was who he was. And what he was most of all was an example."[1]

Like a Mighty Boulder

A child who grows up with strong role models and positive examples for living is blessed indeed. A recent Gallup Poll reported that, among thirteen- to seventeen-year-olds, 51 percent said that they have no role models to look up to in life. The other 49 percent cited their parents—not celebrities—as role models whom they wanted to emulate.[2]

As I looked at this information, I realized that in my own life it was my mother's kindness, generosity, and continual self-giving that had the greatest impact on my life. She was and continues to be an inspiration and role model for my life, though she's been with the Lord for many years. To this day, I look to her example for inspiration when I am facing choices and challenges in my life.

If you want to influence one life or thousands, there is nothing more powerful than a positive example. Whether you are a parent, a teacher, a student, a preacher, a business leader, or an employee, you can and should live to be an example to others. If you live to impact and influence others in a positive way, your example will make its mark—even though the effect of your example on others may not be appreciated until years or even decades later.

Someone is watching you wherever you are—at school, at work, at church, in the neighborhood, or at home. People are learning from your life example, and you may not even know it. In fact, that person who is watching you may not be fully aware of how much your example is influencing his or her life.

But a day will come when that person looks back and remembers you and says, "This person's example made the difference in my life. I am who I am because this person was an example to me."

Young people sometimes come to me and say, "I feel called by God to full-time ministry. Which seminary should I apply to? Which offers the best training for my future ministry?"

I always have one standard piece of advice: "Don't focus only on the academic record of a seminary. Don't focus only on the size of the student body, or the prestige of the professors, or the traditions, history, and reputation of the institution.

Focus instead on the godliness of the professors. Ask people who know the school and its professors, 'What kind of examples do they set? What kinds of role models are they? What kind of impact do they make on the lives of the students who pass through their classrooms?' The knowledge a professor imparts may be quickly forgotten, but the life of a great teacher will affect you forever."

Regardless your age or station in life, people are watching you to see how you handle stress, temptation, opposition, unfair treatment, and disappointment. They notice if an overbearing boss, a rude customer, or an unfair teacher causes you to bless or to curse. They notice if you speak well of others or if you are the office gossip. They notice if you cut ethical corners or if you maintain Christlike integrity.

People are impacted by your life far more than your words. They are influenced more by your actions than by your instructions. They absorb your lifestyle more than your hairstyle. They will emulate your walk more than your talk. Rev. Claude Wisdom White penned these words:

> A careful man I ought to be;
>> A little fellow follows me.
> I do not dare to go astray
>> For fear he'll go the selfsame way.
> I cannot once escape his eyes;
>> Whate'er he sees me do he tries.
> Like me he says he's going to be,
>> This little chap who follows me.
> He thinks that I am good and fine,
>> Believes in every word of mine.
> The base in me he must not see,
>> That little chap who follows me.
> I must remember as I go
>> Through summer's sun and winter's snow,

I'm building for the years to be,
That little chap who follows me.

That is the very message Paul brings to us in the eighth of
the fifteen secrets of positive living. In 2 Corinthians 6, Paul
tells us he is confident of the fact he has exemplified and modeled Christ in his life. Confident of this fact, Paul in turn offers
his life as a role model for others to follow.

How can Paul say that? Is he prideful and boastful? Let me
tell you something: For many years when I was a young pastor, 2 Corinthians 6 troubled me greatly. Whenever I read it, I
wanted to get away from it very quickly, because Paul's words
sounded arrogant to my ears.

But today I understand much more clearly what Paul is saying and why he says it. As my walk with the Lord strengthened
and I better understood the Scriptures, I began to understand
why being a positive example to others gives a Christian the
power of positive living. In this passage, Paul confidently tells
the Corinthian believers, "We put no stumbling block in anyone's path, so that our ministry will not be discredited. Rather,
as servants of God we commend ourselves in every way" (2
Cor. 6:3–4a).

Paul was so confident that his life had been molded and
shaped by Christ that he boldly tells people, in effect, "Now,
you look at me and model your life after mine, because I have
modeled my life after Christ. Through my behavior and my
ministry, I commend myself to you as an example for you to
follow."

Serving Christ and living as a role model before others gave
Paul the power to live above the false accusations of those who
hated him; power to live above the anguish of his soul; power
to live above the deep hurts and disappointments of life common to us all. The one thing no one can successfully attack in
your life is the power of your example. People can lie about

you and twist your words, but they can't attack your positive example. The godly example of your life is like a huge boulder ripping through the tissue of their false accusations. It's like a fortress deflecting all their arrows or like a mountain they cannot scale.

The great medical missionary Albert Schweitzer once said, "Example is not the *main* thing in influencing others. It's the *only* thing." The exemplary life Paul has lived as a follower of Christ has been his strongest defense against his enemies. That's why, in the middle of his most trying days, Paul kept going strong.

The fact that God was using Paul as an example to others brought him comfort and endurance. He could persevere through trials and afflictions, knowing people were watching his example and learning to stand strong for God through the power of his example. He could praise God in the midst of the prison, knowing God was using Paul's prison experiences to build up the faith of all those who were watching his example.

How to Set an Example for Others

How did Paul practice the power of example? Setting an example for others is one of the hardest things in the world to do. It's much easier to say, "Do as I say" than "Do as I do." It's much easier to set rules than to set a good example. Paul knew that—so in these verses, he tells us how we can set a good example for others to follow, just as he did. In this passage of 2 Corinthians, he gives us a practical three-part plan for living as Christian role models:

1. Live in partnership with God (2 Cor. 6:1–10).
2. Practice the love of God (2 Cor. 6:11–13).
3. Persistently obey the injunction of God (2 Cor. 6:14–7:1).

Each of us is either setting a good example for others by the life we lead—or we are setting obstacles in front of others. There is no middle ground. We have to decide which kind of example we shall be—an example of Christ and His life, or a false example that leads others astray and gives people a false impression of Christ and His life. So let's look at each part of Paul's three-part plan for living as a Christian role model.

God's Fellow Workers

First, *live in partnership with God.* Paul writes, "As God's fellow workers we urge you not to receive God's grace in vain" (2 Cor. 6:1). It's impossible to set a consistently good example in our own power. Only in partnership with God can we succeed. That is why Paul says we are "God's fellow workers," partners with God.

Many people say, "I don't want to be a role model. I don't want other people watching my behavior. I don't want the pressure of knowing people are patterning themselves after my example." Other people say, "Being a role model is too confining. I want to be able to let loose and indulge in certain sins. I can't be an authentic role model, so I'll just have to fake it. When I'm in public, I'll act like a role model—but when I'm in private, I'll live to please myself."

Friend in Christ, you are in partnership with God—and that is not a burden, that is a privilege. You don't need to fake being a role model. You simply need to realize that living by the power of example is a joy, not a chore. God, your partner, the Creator of heaven and earth, will sustain you when you feel inadequate. He will lift you up when you feel down.

When you willingly live in partnership with God, you'll discover you are no longer tormented by the disparity between the "public" you and the "private" you. You don't have to live in fear of being found out. You know exactly who you are and you're comfortable in your own skin. You live by the power of the Holy Spirit instead of your own faltering strength. Instead of wearing different "masks" for different occasions, you live authentically and transparently, so the life of Christ is manifest in you.

Paul goes on to write:

> We put no stumbling block in anyone's path, so that our ministry will not be discredited. Rather, as servants of God we commend ourselves in every way: in great endurance; in troubles, hardships and distresses; in beatings, imprisonments and riots; in hard work, sleepless nights and hunger; in purity, understanding, patience and kindness; in the Holy Spirit and in sincere love; in truthful speech and in the power of God; with weapons of righteousness in the right hand and in the left; through glory and dishonor, bad report and good report; genuine, yet regarded as impostors; known, yet regarded as unknown; dying, and yet we live on; beaten, and yet not killed; sorrowful, yet always rejoicing; poor, yet making many rich; having nothing, and yet possessing everything.
>
> *2 Corinthians 6:3-10*

Notice that statement in verse 4: "as servants of God we commend ourselves in every way . . ." Paul did not say he commends himself as an example because of his academic degrees, or his bank account, or his professional status. He commends himself as *a servant of God*. His focus is not on being an example in terms of earthly accomplishments, but in terms of his partnership with God.

When does this life of partnership with God manifest itself? Only when everything is going well? When the sun is shining in your life? When you are successful and all is going well? Absolutely not! Hear how Paul commends himself as an example to others:

In troubles, hardships, and distresses. In beatings, imprisonments, and riots. In hard work, sleepless nights, and hunger. In times of being dishonored, slandered, treated as an impostor, and ignored. In experiences of being mistreated nearly to death. In conditions of poverty, sorrow, and deprivation. In other words, Paul is saying, "No matter what life throws at me, it cannot defeat me because *I am in partnership with God*. And as God's fellow worker, I choose to exhibit an exemplary life by His power, regardless my difficulties and afflictions. Through Him, I am victorious over all these things."

Someone once said Christians are like tea bags—you only find out how strong they are when they're in hot water. Anyone can sing in the sunshine, but when you can sing during the storm, when the wind is blowing in your face, *that's* when you know you are in true partnership with God.

The Cold Shoulder

Second, *practice the love of God*. The power of example is only possible when you practice the love of God. Paul writes: "We have spoken freely to you, Corinthians, and opened wide our hearts to you. We are not withholding our affection from you, but you are withholding yours from us. As a fair exchange—I speak as to my children—open wide your hearts also" (2 Cor. 6:11–13).

Have you ever gotten the cold shoulder from someone? Some say the expression "cold shoulder" originated this way: In medieval England, people would travel for days to visit friends and relatives, and they would often stay and visit for a week or longer. If a guest overstayed his welcome, the host had a way of letting his guest know it was time for him to go home. The host would serve a roasted lamb. While everyone else would get a nice, hot piece of lamb to eat, the unwelcome guest would get a specific piece of unappetizing meat: the cold shoulder. Most guests quickly took the hint.

Nowadays, the "cold shoulder" refers to someone snubbing you or treating you unkindly. When someone gives you the cold shoulder, how do you feel about that person? You probably don't feel very warm and fuzzy. It's hard to continue loving a person who lets you know you are not welcome, that you are disliked and rejected.

Years ago, when I was thirty years old, a man worked for me. He was twenty-seven years older than me.

When I arrived on the scene in my leadership position, he behaved in a cold, distant manner toward me. No matter how friendly I tried to be toward him, I could see a coldness in his eyes. Oh, he would often wear a smile—but his eyes betrayed his true feelings. He resented me and I didn't know why.

I became increasingly troubled over this man. I wanted to react in the flesh. I thought, *I've never done anything to this man! What is his problem?*

Finally, I prayed about this problem and I sought God with all my heart. Then I went to the man and said, "I have nothing toward you but Christian love and respect. But you are angry with me and I don't understand why. Please tell me what's wrong."

We talked—and I learned that someone gave this man some totally erroneous information about me. We were able to correct his mistaken impression. Once he knew the truth, we became good friends and coworkers for many years.

Twenty-six years later, this brother went to be with the Lord. I sent a note of sympathy and remembrance to his widow, and she wrote back, saying, "Though he was many years your senior, he looked up to you and admired you."

I wept as I read those words. I realized I came very close to shutting this man out by reacting in the flesh—and in doing so, I would have made a terrible mess of things. But God in His grace moved me to respond in His love, reaching out to solve the problem in our relationship. The result was, this man and I had more than a quarter of a century of friendship and partnership together before he went to be with the Lord.

I don't tell this story to serve myself and my own ego. In truth, I came perilously close to doing great harm to God's purpose in this man's life and my own. But God very graciously urged me to practice His love. This story is a constant reminder to me to continually practice the love of God in all my relationships.

Sometimes people hate us and resent us simply because they have received the wrong information. This is precisely what happened in Corinth. False apostles spread false accusations about Paul. They said Paul was only interested in promoting his own agenda. They claimed Paul didn't truly love the Corinthians—that he was a false and untrustworthy friend to them. As a result of the gossip the false teachers spread about Paul, his friends in Corinth became cold and distant toward him. They gave Paul the cold shoulder.

Perhaps you can now see, if you've never seen it before, why the sin of gossip is so frequently condemned in Scripture. There are few sins that cause more hurt and suffering within churches, within families, within the workplace, than the sin of gossip. If people come to you with a juicy bit of gossip, *stop them!* Say, "Let's go to that person together and find out if this is true or not. Let's not engage in the sin of gossip."

You cannot read 2 Corinthians without feeling the anguish of this man. Paul suffered greatly from the effects of gossip. These rumors, spread by the false teachers, were causing some of Paul's friends to withhold affection. They were giving him the cold shoulder. Make no mistake—it's painful to be lied about. Sometimes we would prefer to just slink away, crawl into a hole, pull the hole in after us, and just not deal with it.

But it is *vital* we deal with it. We're under an obligation to set an example—and that means we must set the record straight. When you are motivated by love for God and His people, then you must deal with the issues that arise. You must lovingly confront those who sin against you.

There are times, of course, when you can't do anything about the situation. Sometimes people choose not to be reconciled, no matter what you do. Keep loving that person, keep reaching out, then wait for God's timing.

Look at Paul's description of the essence of real love: First, there must be honesty. Paul writes, "We have spoken freely to you, Corinthians, and opened wide our hearts to you." Second, there must be continuous affection regardless of behavior. He writes, "We are not withholding our affection from you, but you are withholding yours from us." Third, we must continuously seek fellowship with the other person. Paul writes, "As a fair exchange—I speak as to my children—open wide your hearts also."

If the great apostle Paul was not too proud to open his heart and let the Corinthian Christians see he was hurting, then who are we to hide our hurts from someone who perceives us erroneously and treats us unjustly?

Persistently Obeying the Injunction of God

Third, *persistently obey the injunction of God*. The power of example is only possible when you persistently obey the injunction of God. Paul writes:

> Do not be yoked together with unbelievers. For what do righteousness and wickedness have in common? Or what fellowship can light have with darkness? What harmony is there between Christ and Belial? What does a believer have in common with an unbeliever? What agreement is there between the temple of God and idols? For we are the temple of the living God. As God

has said: "I will live with them and walk among them, and I will be their God, and they will be my people."

> "Therefore come out from them
>   and be separate, says the Lord.
> Touch no unclean thing,
>   and I will receive you."
> "I will be a Father to you,
>   and you will be my sons and daughters,
>   says the Lord Almighty."

Since we have these promises, dear friends, let us purify ourselves from everything that contaminates body and spirit, perfecting holiness out of reverence for God.

(2 Corinthians 6:14-7:1)

Paul begins by saying, "Do not be yoked together with unbelievers." This passage has been tragically misinterpreted over the years. Some have taken this to mean we Christians should totally cut ourselves off from unbelievers. That is *not* what Paul is saying. How can we share the good news of Jesus Christ with others if we cut ourselves off from them?

Clearly, God wants us to be in the world, sharing the message of hope with those who have no hope. Yet, while we are in the world, He wants us to be different from the world, so lost people will see that Jesus Christ makes all the difference in our lives. So we must not shut ourselves off from unbelievers. We must not refuse to associate with them—but we must maintain our uniqueness as Christians.

When Paul says, "Do not be yoked together with unbelievers," he is referring to Deuteronomy 22:10, where God said to Israel, "Do not plow with an ox and a donkey yoked together." Why did God issue such a command? The answer goes deeper than merely forbidding cruelty to animals. God was giving Israel a spiritual principle through this picture of an ox and donkey under the same yoke.

These two animals do not have the same nature or the same strength. If you place them together under a common yoke, the stronger animal will pull ahead, the weaker animal will lag, the work will not be done well, and both animals will suffer. This is a picture of two people being joined together who do not belong together, who are spiritually mismatched.

I was once asked to serve on an evangelism committee of one of the mainline denominations. When I met with the committee, I discovered most of the members of that committee defined "evangelism" differently than I did. To them, "evangelism" means recruiting new members to the church, just as a country club would recruit new members.

My own definition is the Bible's definition. The word comes from the New Testament Greek word *"euangelion,"* meaning *good news*. So "evangelism," according to the Bible, means telling people the good news of Jesus Christ and making disciples. After a couple of meetings, I came to the conclusion these people and I were unequally yoked. They were pulling one way, I was pulling another—so I resigned from that committee.

I know of a young man who loved a young woman—and she loved him as well. One day, he proposed marriage to her. She didn't take any time to consider the young man's proposal. She looked him in the eye and said, "I can't marry you. I would be disobeying God's injunction. You aren't a believer, and I cannot be unequally yoked with an unbeliever."

This young man was baffled by what she said. He had never heard of such a principle. He thought all any marriage needed was romantic love—yet here was this young woman telling him love was *not* enough. They both had to be followers of Christ.

The young woman had an opportunity to witness to this young man. And I can tell you this man is a strong follower of

Christ today. Why? Because God honored the young woman's desire to obey the injunction of God, "Do not be yoked together with unbelievers."

Paul is saying it's impossible for a believer and a nonbeliever to have the same spiritual goals. Trying to mix the two is as absurd as saying that light can have fellowship with darkness, righteousness with lawlessness, Christ with Satan. The two do not mix.

You cannot experience positive living unless you are living as an example to others. You cannot be an example without living in partnership with God. You cannot be an example without practicing the love of God. And you cannot be an example without persistent obedience to the injunctions of God.

General George C. Marshall was secretary of state in the aftermath of World War II. In 1953, he won the Nobel Peace Prize for his work in promoting the postwar reconstruction of Europe—an effort known as the Marshall Plan. Before World War II, General Marshall commanded the Infantry School at Fort Benning, Georgia.

When General Marshall first arrived at Fort Benning, he found the entire post in a generally deplorable and run-down condition. Many military leaders would simply line the soldiers up, reprimand them sharply, and order them to clean up the place. But General Marshall didn't work that way. He didn't bark any orders. He simply requisitioned a can of paint and a paintbrush, a rake and a hoe, a hammer and some nails, and he began working on his own personal quarters.

The general didn't say a word to his men. He didn't have to. The officers and men on his own block saw the general sprucing up his own quarters, and they followed his example. Soon, the officers and men on the surrounding blocks also did the same. Within a few weeks, the entire post had been repaired, painted, weeded, raked, and cleaned up.

That's the power of example.

Sorrow: The Back Door to Happiness

George Matheson was a brilliant and accomplished student at the University of Glasgow, Scotland, despite being almost completely blind. After graduation, he planned to marry his fiancée and attend seminary, then spend the rest of his life as a husband and pastor. Soon after his graduation, however, his fiancée told him, "George, I can't be the wife of a blind preacher." And she left him.

Though deeply wounded after being abandoned by the woman he loved, Matheson went on to seminary and was ordained to the ministry in 1868. He was called to serve as pastor of a church in the seaside village of Innellan, Scotland. Years went by. George Matheson thought the pain of his fiancée's rejection was in the past.

In 1882, when Matheson was forty, his sister announced her wedding.

2 Corinthians 7:2–16

Though George Matheson was happy for his little sister, the event threw him into a deep depression. The joyous festivities reminded him of all he lost when his own beloved abandoned him. The night of the wedding, he experienced, in his words, "the most severe mental suffering."

Yet that same night, George Matheson felt God speaking to him and giving him the words of a song. And George Matheson began to write about a love very different from the love of his lost fiancée. Her love failed him and let him go. But the love of God, he realized, would never let him go.

Looking back on the writing of that song, he recalled, "I had the impression of having it dictated to me by some inward voice rather than of working it out myself. I am quite sure that the whole work was completed in five minutes. . . . It came like a dayspring from on high."[1] The words God gave to George Matheson were these:

> O Love that wilt not let me go,
> I rest my weary soul in thee;
> I give thee back the life I owe,
> That in thine ocean depths its flow
> May richer, fuller be.
>
> O Joy that seekest me through pain,
> I cannot close my heart to thee;
> I trace the rainbow through the rain,
> And feel the promise is not vain
> That morn shall tearless be.

Out of George Matheson's sorrow came a message of a love that never lets us go. Out of his physical blindness came a vision of a rainbow glimpsed through the rain.

There are few experiences more painful than the experience of a broken relationship, with its sense of rejection, abandonment, and hopelessness. When we feel pain, our tendency is to find a way to medicate it. We want a pill, an injection, a magic potion, to make the pain go away.

But there is no instant cure for the pain of broken trust, promises betrayed, estrangement, and rejection. When a loved one says, "I don't love you anymore," or a child says, "I hate you," or a trusted friend betrays you and walks away from you, what do you do? When sorrow comes crashing through the front door of your life . . .

Can you still find a back door to happiness?

Two Ways of Dealing with Sorrow

There are only two ways of dealing with painful life experiences inflicted on us by other people. One of these two approaches leads to happiness; the other does not. This first response—the one that leads to happiness—is:

- recognizing the hurt people cause us is the result of sin and wrongdoing
- identifying sin and wrongdoing
- providing an opportunity for repentance and reconciliation.

If we will follow these three steps, we are able to use our sorrow and suffering as a doorway to happiness, restoration, and understanding. What is the alternative to this approach? Simply this:

Do nothing. Allow the sorrow, pain, and resentment to eat into your soul like a corrosive acid. Let it go on and on for as long as you live. Never deal with it. Never let go of it. Never get over it.

That is the approach to sorrow and pain described by Stephen Crane in his 1895 poem "The Heart":

In the desert
I saw a creature, naked, bestial,
Who, squatting upon the ground,
Held his heart in his hands,
And ate of it.

I said, "Is it good, friend?"
"It is bitter—bitter," he answered;
"But I like it
Because it is bitter,
And because it is my heart."

Two ways of dealing with sorrow. Both involve pain. The first requires us to experience the temporary pain that comes with healing and deliverance. It is the sort of short-term pain we experience when we go through surgery. After the pain is over, we are healthy and whole.

The second produces a pain that is a prolonged, chronic, and even lifelong condition. It is like an untreated wound that festers and throbs and never heals.

What destroys most relationships? Small misunderstandings. A hasty word. A thoughtless action. False information—a rumor that misleads and unfairly destroys an innocent reputation. An unresolved argument.

In 1995, my wife and I visited a friend who lives in St. Andrews, Scotland. My host took me to see an ancient church building—one of the most beautiful stone and stained-glass structures I have ever seen. As I stood there admiring that beautiful house of worship, my friend said, "You know, only a dozen or so people ever attend this church on Sunday mornings—and they are all senior citizens. The building is magnificent, but the church itself is dying."

Then he proceeded to tell me one of the most heart-wrenching stories I ever heard. He said, "The minister and the organist in this church have not talked to each other for years. A long time ago, they had a falling-out and they haven't spoken to each other since. This feud has been going on for so many years that when I tried to get them together to forgive each other, neither of them could remember the cause of the estrangement. But at the same time, neither would forgive the other."

I said, "But how do they cooperate on the worship service? They have to talk to each other to plan the service, don't they?"

"They have found a way around having to talk to each other," my host said. "The minister comes in early, before the organist arrives, and he places the sermon title on the organ. Then the organist comes in, selects the hymns, and places a sheet of paper with the hymn numbers on the minister's desk while the minister is out of his office.

"At the time this feud began, the church was filled with worshippers every Sunday. Since the minister and the organist became estranged, attendance has dwindled to a dozen or less every Sunday morning."

What a tragedy! There are few more destructive forces in a church, family, or workplace than unresolved conflict. The Bible gives us only one way to restore joy, peace, and God's blessing when a relationship has been broken by conflict. The biblical way is to *courageously confront* the brokenness, deal with the conflict, and heal the relationships through the love and forgiveness of Jesus Christ. That is the godly, healthy approach to sorrow and pain. If you are trying to avoid the pain of dealing with conflict in your life, then the pain will only deepen. It will not go away.

Worse, unresolved conflict—especially between Christians—opens the door for Satan to come in and gain a stronghold in our lives. It disrupts our ability to hear the voice of God's Spirit. It destroys the ministry of God through us, just as the effectiveness of that church in St. Andrews was reduced to almost nil.

A gifted surgeon in our church once told me many patients come to him with excruciating pain, but he can find no physiological reason. Medical science tells us some illnesses are caused not by physical and organic disorders, but by mental and emotional processes such as anger, anxiety, depression, and guilt. These illnesses are called "psychosomatic" or "psychophysiologic" disorders, and they are more common than most of us realize. Physicians know these disorders commonly occur during times when a person is experiencing problems with relationships.

I'm personally convinced that unresolved conflict, broken friendships, and troubled church and family relationships can lead to real physical pain. Emotional suffering can produce physical suffering. Yet, Paul, in 2 Corinthians 7, wants us to know that sorrow can truly provide an unexpected back door to happiness—if we respond to our sorrows and suffering in a godly and healthy way.

Paul's Distress and Anguish

The apostle Paul experienced many forms of suffering and sorrow. He was beaten, stoned, and flogged nearly to death—not once but multiple times. However, none of these experiences troubled and distressed Paul as much as when his friends believed the lies and gossip of his enemies. Imagine: Paul's own friends were willing to believe the worst about him. They turned on him, rejected him, and insulted him—all because of false rumors spread by false teachers.

Paul must have wondered, *Why didn't any of them defend me? Why did they believe lies about me and close their hearts to me?* Understand, Paul was not just being sensitive or thin-skinned. The believers in Corinth owed their salvation to the preaching of the apostle Paul. Before he came to that city, the people of Corinth were pagans and idol worshippers. He founded the church and personally led many of the Corinthians to Christ. They were his spiritual children—yet they chose to believe a lie about their spiritual father. Their rejection and betrayal must have wounded him deeply.

Imagine your own son or daughter, your spouse, your business partner, your closest friend, believing a lying rumor—then spreading that rumor to others. That is the kind of bewildering pain the apostle was suffering.

Paul was so deeply hurt that he wrote them a tough and confrontational letter. In it, he told the Corinthians he would never return to Corinth again. After all, why should he subject himself to further emotional pain? On an emotional level, the writing of this confrontational letter was a painful experience, and Paul didn't want to do it. But on a spiritual level, Paul knew he had to do it.

I must tell you, I hate confrontation. If it were purely up to me, I would never confront anyone about anything. I'm a peace-loving fellow. But I will confront people when I have to for the sake of the gospel, for the sake of Jesus Christ, and for the sake of His church. I suspect Paul probably had similar feelings about confrontation. He didn't enjoy it, he wasn't eager to do it, but he confronted sin when he had to, out of obedience to God.

Earlier in this letter, Paul told the Corinthians, "For I wrote you out of great distress and anguish of heart and with many tears, not to grieve you but to let you know the depth of my love for you" (2 Cor. 2:4). So we know the previous letter, the confrontational letter, was as painful for Paul to write as it was for the Corinthian Christians to read.

Paul sent the letter with Titus, his trusted lieutenant and fellow worker. Then Paul went to Macedonia, where he anxiously awaited their response. Have you ever been in that position? Have you ever sent someone a difficult message, then waited anxiously for the results? You wondered, *How will the other person respond? In anger? In repentance? In bitterness? In remorse?* The whole time you are waiting for the other person's answer, you are in suspense.

Paul knew the Corinthians could have responded in one of two ways, as we saw earlier. They could have sent a letter to Paul saying, "Who do you think you are, Paul? We are right! You are wrong! How dare you confront us this way?" They could have hardened their hearts against Paul—and in so doing, they would have chosen the chronic pain of stubbornly refusing to repent.

Or . . . they could have come under the conviction of the Holy Spirit. They could have read the apostle's words and realized their error. They could have apologized to Paul for doubting him, for believing the whispers of Paul's enemies instead of the bold voice of Paul himself. They could have responded in repentance and remorse for the anguish they caused him.

While waiting in Macedonia for the Corinthians' response, Paul was plagued by worry. In 2 Corinthians 7:5, he described his state of mind: "For when we came into Macedonia, this body of ours had no rest, but we were harassed at every turn—conflicts on the outside, fears within."

Why was Paul so conflicted and full of fear? In large part, it was because he was worried about the Corinthians. He was anxious to know what choice they would make. Would they close their hearts against Paul—or would they seek to heal the relationship with the apostle? Paul knew choosing not to reconcile would prolong the pain on both sides—and it would bring spiritual harm to the Corinthians.

Paul sets an example for us in how we should deal with people who turn against us or reject us. We lovingly and honestly confront the issue head-on. We speak the truth in love. Our goal is not to grieve the other person but to let him or her know the depth of our love and our commitment to restoring the relationship. Then—we wait for the other person to respond. At that point, the other person can respond by forgiving and being forgiven—or by rejecting your attempt at reconciliation. It may end beautifully or it may end badly. The important thing is for you to act in obedience and do whatever you can to bring about peace and reconciliation.

You might say, "But, Michael, you just don't understand my problems. You don't know how bad my marriage is. You don't know how impossible it is to live with my spouse." Or, "You don't know how hurtful my parents can be. You didn't hear what they did to me." You're right, I don't know your specific circumstances—but I do know this: there is nothing you are facing today that has not been faced by countless other people.

There is an ancient Arabic proverb that says, "Marriage starts out with a prince kissing an angel—but it ends with a bald-headed man staring across the table at a fat woman." And the philosopher Socrates warned his students to find a good wife to marry. "If you marry a bad wife," he said, "you will become a philosopher!" (Socrates should have warned women to marry a good man—because if they marry a philosopher, they will be miserable.)

Young people often think that once they get married, their problems are over; those who are older and wiser know that some of the most difficult problems in life *begin* with marriage. So if you want to stay married and have a joyful life, you had better learn all you can about how to forgive, how to seek forgiveness, and how to be reconciled with one another. Don't run away from a broken relationship.

If you think, "I can bail out of this relationship and find a better one," chances are you will repeat the same pattern in your next relationship. Going from relationship to relationship just means you are spreading the misery to more and more people. Moving on won't make you happy, so stop running. Deal with the relationship you are in right now. Resolve the conflict and find healing in your relationship.

Let pain and sorrow be your back door to joy and happiness. That is one of the most important secrets of positive living.

A Surgical Pain

What if you go to the other person for reconciliation, but he or she refuses to deal with the issue? Well, you can't force people to do what they refuse to do. Human beings have free will. You are only responsible for your side of the equation. As Paul wrote to the Romans, "If it is possible, as far as it depends on you, live at peace with everyone" (Rom. 12:18).

There are some people you simply can't get along with. What do you do with people like that? Well, you keep your heart open to them. You never know when they may see the light. Let go of any bitterness toward them, forgive them, and get on with your life. Confess your sins to the Lord and don't let anger, resentment, or guilt clog up the lines of communication between you and God. You may not always be able to have a restored and reconciled relationship with other people, but you can always restore your relationship with the Lord.

There is good news in the story of the broken relationship between Paul and the Corinthians. The believers in Corinth were moved by Paul's letter—and they reconciled with him. Paul wrote:

> But God, who comforts the downcast, comforted us by the coming of Titus, and not only by his coming but also by the comfort you had given him. He told us about your longing for me, your deep sorrow, your ardent concern for me, so that my joy was greater than ever.
>
> Even if I caused you sorrow by my letter, I do not regret it. Though I did regret it—I see that my letter hurt you, but only for a little while—yet now I am happy, not because you were made sorry, but because your sorrow led you to repentance. For you became sorrowful as God intended and so were not harmed in any way by us.
>
> *(2 Corinthians 7:6-9)*

Paul said, in effect, "Though my letter caused you temporary sorrow, it resulted in permanent healing—so I don't regret it. Oh, I wish that letter had not needed to be so painful to write and to read—but I rejoice because you chose to open your hearts, not harden them. When I wrote that letter, it was as if I were a surgeon and you were a patient on the operating table. I hated to make an incision that would cause you pain—yet I'm glad I cut out the cancer that was killing our relationship. Had I not done so, our relationship would have died."

Now, if the Corinthians had chosen not to reconcile with Paul, what would Paul have done? Nothing. He did all he could do by confronting the Corinthians with their sin and error against him. He had no power over them. He could not force them to reconcile. Had the Corinthians chosen to continue believing the lies of the false teachers and spreading those lies about Paul, they would have forfeited the blessings God wanted to give them. Paul was concerned not only for his own peace of mind. He was concerned that the Corinthians not miss out on God's blessings.

Thank God, the believers in Corinth chose to reconcile with Paul of their own free will. They chose to receive the blessing of healing, reconciliation, and forgiveness.

Two Kinds of Sorrow

Paul talks about two kinds of sorrow in this passage: worldly sorrow and godly sorrow. He writes, "Godly sorrow brings repentance that leads to salvation and leaves no regret, but worldly sorrow brings death" (2 Cor. 7:10). Worldly sorrow is regret and remorse—the feeling that says, "Oh, I wish nobody knew about this." Paul says this form of sorrow has no healing power, no redemptive value. But godly sorrow leads to true repentance and produces unspeakable joy.

In Jewish weddings, the bridegroom breaks a wineglass

beneath his shoe. Then the guests shout "Mazel tov!" ("Good luck! Congratulations!") and clap their hands. The couple often keeps the broken glass in a velvet pouch as a reminder.

What does the broken glass symbolize? There are several traditions to explain the broken glass. One says it symbolizes the destruction of the Temple in Jerusalem. Another tradition says the broken glass reminds us happy times are special experiences, and we should appreciate them and not waste them. Perhaps the deepest symbolism of all is the tradition that says the shattered glass is a reminder to the couple to closely guard their sacred relationship. Why? Because in that culture, the people believed the marriage relationship, once broken, could never be restored.

In the New Testament, we see that the cross of Calvary stands as the symbol of the restored relationship between God and man. If that relationship can be restored, then any relationship can be restored. The key to a redeemed and healed relationship is that our sorrow must be godly sorrow, not worldly sorrow. Godly sorrow brings true repentance, which leads to salvation and leaves no regret. Worldly sorrow, which is regret without repentance, brings only death—the death of the relationship, the death that comes from unrepented sin.

From time to time, we all experience the sorrow of broken relationships. As long as we refuse to confess our sin, repent of it, and receive forgiveness, there can be no reconciliation. As long as we avoid the temporary surgical pain of confronting sin—whether our own sin or that of the one who sinned against us—we prolong the pain of resentment and brokenness.

Today, you can say, "Lord Jesus, examine my life. Show me where there is sin in my life. Show me where there are relationships I have broken, people I hurt, and sorrows I caused. Show me my error, Lord. Fill me with a desire to repent and reconcile. Open the door of my sorrow and lead me into the joy that comes from having peace with You and peace with others. Amen."

Getting Through Giving

Scientists tell us the realm of nature is riddled with paradox. What is a paradox? It's an idea that appears to be absurd or self-contradictory, but it actually expresses a profound truth.

One of the great paradoxes of science involves the question "What is light?" If you subject a ray of light to certain experiments, light seems to be a particle. But under a different set of experiments, light seems to be a wave. Logically, light cannot be both a particle and a wave—yet the experiments tell us light transcends logic. It's a paradox, beyond the ability of even a physicist to explain.

Just as science is riddled with paradoxes, so is the Christian faith. No other religion is as rich in paradox as biblical Christianity—or even compares with it. I see paradox as one of the great

2 Corinthians 8:1–9

validations of Christianity, because it demonstrates to us that the same God Who created the universe, with all of its natural paradoxes, also created the spiritual realm, with its many spiritual paradoxes.

Yet the very paradoxical nature of the Christian faith often causes people to stumble over Christianity and reject its message. For example, our Muslim friends can neither comprehend nor accept the idea that there can be one God in three persons, nor can they accept the cornerstone of our faith, the fact that God the Creator became a man, Jesus of Nazareth, who lived and died and rose again. Surely, that is the greatest paradox of Scripture—and it is from this one paradox that all other biblical paradoxes are born.

Most of the great paradoxes of Scripture came from the lips of Jesus Himself. He said, "Blessed are the meek, for they will inherit the earth" (Matt. 5:5); "If anyone wants to be first, he must be the very last, and the servant of all" (Mark 9:35); and "For whoever wants to save his life will lose it" (Luke 9:24)—to list just a few.

Dr. James Allen Francis, in his book *The Real Jesus And Other Sermons* (Judson Press, 1926), observed that the entire life of Jesus was a bundle of paradoxes:

> He was born in an obscure village, the child of a peasant woman. He grew up in another obscure village. He worked in a carpenter shop until he was thirty, and then for three years was an itinerant preacher.
>
> He never wrote a book. He never held an office. He never owned a home. He never had a family. He never went to college. . . . He never traveled two hundred miles from the place where He was born. He never did one of the things that usually accompany greatness. . . .
>
> While still a young man, the tide of popular opinion turned against Him. His friends ran away. One of them denied him.

Another betrayed Him. He was turned over to His enemies. He went through the mockery of a trial. He was nailed upon the cross between two thieves. His executioners gambled for the only piece of property He had on earth while He was dying, and that was His coat. When He was dead, He was taken down and laid in a borrowed grave through the pity of a friend.

Nineteen long centuries have come and gone and today He is the center of the human race and the leader of the column of progress. . . . All the armies that ever marched, and all the navies that were ever built, and all the parliaments that ever sat and all the kings that ever reigned, put together, have not affected the life of man upon the earth as powerfully as has this one solitary life.

A paradox violates common sense—yet it reveals truth as grand and unshakable as the Rock of Gibraltar. As we come to Paul's tenth secret for positive living, we encounter one of the most powerful and life-changing paradoxes of Scripture: getting through giving. Like every other paradox, this one confounds logic—yet it's absolutely true.

"I'll Die a Rich Man"

The natural mind says, "If you want to get something, you've got to grab for it, you've got to take it. If you want to get ahead in life, you've got to push everyone else out of your way. Nice guys finish last. Don't worry how many people you have to step on to get what you want—just look out for Number One. It's a dog-eat-dog world out there. So make sure you are the biggest, meanest, hungriest dog in the junkyard."

That's the law of the jungle. That's the logic of this world.

But the spiritual paradox Paul gives us in this secret of positive living violates the law of the jungle and confounds the logic of this world. Paul says, in effect, "The world is wrong. You don't get by taking. You get by giving."

Sometime ago, I read about a British ship, the *Britannia,* which sank off the coast of Brazil. The hold of the ship was filled with kegs of Spanish gold coins. The crew, hoping to save the gold, brought the kegs of gold up onto the deck. Meanwhile, the sea was pounding the ship, causing it to break up quickly. The sailors had to abandon their effort to save the gold and settle for saving their lives.

As the last men aboard scrambled into the last of the lifeboats, a young midshipman was sent back to make sure no sailors were left behind. He dashed to the main deck—and to his amazement, he found a sailor sitting on the deck with gold coins heaped all around him. He had broken into a few kegs and spilled out the gold, and was running his fingers through the piles of gleaming coins—even as the ship was breaking apart and settling into the waves.

"Get into the lifeboat!" the midshipman called. "You'll drown if you stay on the ship!"

"I've been a poor man all my life!" the sailor shouted back. "Today I'll die a rich man!"

So the midshipman ran back to the lifeboat alone and was saved—and the greedy sailor did indeed die a rich man, for all the good his piles of gold did him.

We hear that story and we think, *What utter foolishness! What insanity! What good is a fortune in gold to a drowning man?*

Yet that is exactly how the natural mind of man operates. Every day, we are surrounded by people whose thinking is no less absurd than the thinking of that "rich" sailor. You've seen them pass you on the freeway in their Jaguars and Mercedes, with a bumper sticker that reads: "He Who Dies With the Most Toys Wins." They are focused on their investment portfolios, their benefit plans, their stock options, and their 401(k)s—but they give no thought to storing up treasures in heaven. They are always thinking about how they can get more and more and more—and they do not understand that the secret for positive living is *getting by giving.*

Pressed Down, Shaken Together, and Running Over

The foundational verse in 2 Corinthians 8 is verse 9, because in this verse Paul highlights Jesus as an example of how we are to live our lives: "For you know the grace of our Lord Jesus Christ, that though he was rich, yet for your sakes he became poor, so that you through his poverty might become rich." Everything Paul writes in this passage is built upon the truth expressed in that verse.

Now, there are some Christians who see giving as an obligation or an imposition or a chore. But Jesus tells us giving is the process by which we activate God's pipeline of blessing. In Luke 6:38, Jesus says, "Give, and it will be given to you. A good measure, pressed down, shaken together and running over, will be poured into your lap. For with the measure you use, it will be measured to you."

Growing up in the Middle East, I saw the practice Jesus describes on a daily basis. In the Middle East, you don't buy grain in plastic packages from a supermarket shelf. You buy from a vendor in the marketplace or in a little shop. The vendor measures the grain in a container and you pay for the grain according to the volume measured out.

Now, a dishonest vendor will use a measuring cup with a false bottom in it, which is designed to give you less grain than you paid for. He tries to increase his profits by overcharging you.

But a generous vendor will actually give you *more* than a legal measurement. He'll shake the measuring cup so that the grain will settle and he can pour more in. Not satisfied with that, he will press the grain down so he can pour still more grain in. Not satisfied with simply filling the cup to the brim, he will actually mound up the grain in the measuring cup so that you get more grain than you paid for. This vendor is giving generously.

Now, that is how God says He will give to us when we give to Him. If we give sacrificially, God will give generously to us. Giving is the secret to activating God's amazing give-back program. It's impossible to outgive God.

But what many Christians have done—to their own hurt—is they have placed a false bottom in the measuring cup when they have given to God. The falseness of their giving was reflected in the meagerness of their getting. They gave begrudgingly rather than cheerfully. They tried to trick God into seeing them as better stewards of His resources than they actually were. This is the height of foolishness, because God sees not only the amount given, but the heart that gives it. You cannot get away with lying to God.

The first deaths reported in the early church involved a couple and their giving. Ananias and Sapphira donated money to the church out of the proceeds from the sale of a piece of real estate. Now, that would have been a laudable act of generosity, except for one thing: they claimed they gave *all* of the proceeds from the sale, when they actually only gave a *portion*. They weren't giving to please God. They were giving to build up their reputation as major donors to the church. In Acts 5:1–11, we see that God dealt severely with their hypocrisy. They paid with their lives for lying to God.

Las Vegas or the Kingdom of God?

Now, some people hear about this principle, "Get by giving," and they think, *Okay, the Bible said to give so I can get. What a deal! Lord, here's a check, here's my giving—and I'm not picky about what form the "getting" takes. If you choose to make me a lottery winner, that's fine with me. If you want me to discover oil in my backyard, just tell me where to drill. Or if you just want to drop bags of gold out of the sky, tell me where to stand so I don't get clobbered.*

So they give and then they wait. A day passes, two days, a week, a month—and their patience wears thin. Nothing's happening! God's let them down. They gave, but they didn't get—so now they're mad at God. And mad at the preacher. And mad at the church.

What's wrong with this picture? The problem is, this person was giving out of the wrong attitude. He was giving selfishly. He was giving to get—and therein lies another paradox. God promises we get by giving—but if we give only to get, then we are giving from the wrong attitude, a selfish motive—and God can't be fooled.

God knows when we are giving merely to manipulate Him into blessing us. He knows when we are treating Him like a slot machine instead of worshipping Him as the Lord of Glory. A person who gives with the selfish motive of getting from God is doomed to disappointment when he puts his money in the collection plate, pulls the lever of prayer—then fails to hear *ka-ching! ka-ching!* People who practice that sort of giving belong in Las Vegas, not the Kingdom of God.

At the beginning of chapter 8, Paul gives us an example of the kind of giver God loves: the Christians of Macedonia. Paul writes:

And now, brothers, we want you to know about the grace that God has given the Macedonian churches. Out of the most severe trial, their overflowing joy and their extreme poverty welled up in rich generosity. For I testify that they gave as much as they were able, and even beyond their ability. Entirely on their own, they urgently pleaded with us for the privilege of sharing in this service to the saints. And they did not do as we expected, but they gave themselves first to the Lord and then to us in keeping with God's will.

(2 Corinthians 8:1-5)

Paul tells the Corinthians that the Macedonian Christians gave joyfully, despite their poverty and difficult circumstances. The Macedonians didn't have much to give, but what they had, they gave eagerly. Giving made the Macedonians happy. The Christians in Macedonia understood the principle of laying up treasures in heaven, and they were confident God would supply all their needs. Their great faith freed them up to give generously—indeed, to give far more than they could reasonably afford.

So Paul told the Corinthians, in effect, "Look at how the Macedonians give. Even in their poverty, they have become a role model for Christian giving." Now we must ask ourselves this question: Where did the Macedonians get the idea of giving so generously, even in the midst of poverty? Answer: they got the idea from Jesus Christ Himself.

Again, we go back to the key verse of this passage: "For you know the grace of our Lord Jesus Christ, that though he was rich, yet for your sakes he became poor, so that you through his poverty might become rich" (2 Cor. 8:9). Whenever there is authentic Christlike love, it will manifest itself in sacrificial giving—for that is how Jesus Christ Himself gave to us.

We often see wealthy celebrities calling for the elimination of poverty. They give a concert here or a speech there to benefit the poor—but they sit on their millions and refuse to put their money where their mouths are. Their talk is just talk. Their giving? They brush the crumbs off their table and donate those crumbs to the poor—and, in return, they receive millions of dollars' worth of free publicity.

Jesus calls us to follow His example and give sacrificially. Giving that does not cost us anything is not true giving.

During a Sunday-morning church service, a man sat staring at the money in his wallet. Meanwhile, the collection plate was coming his way. The usher leaned over to the man and said, "Sir? Is something wrong?"

"I'm just trying to decide what to give," the man with the wallet said. "I suppose I could give five dollars and not feel it."

"Well," the usher said, "why don't you give fifty dollars and *really* feel it?"

God does not want "numb" givers who don't feel their giving. He wants givers who feel excited and ecstatic about giving in a sacrificial way. He wants our giving to cost us dearly, so that we truly *feel* it—and truly feel good about giving back to God. That's how the Macedonians gave. They didn't give their pocket change or the money they found in the sofa cushions. They gave their grocery money and even their rent money. They went without some of the necessities of life in order to give to God—and it made them happy to do so!

They gave out of a desire to be like the Lord Jesus Christ, Who gave up everything for them. He gave up His own life, His glory, His power, and His majesty. What motivated Him to do that? Sheer selfless love! Jesus didn't give up everything to die for perfect people who already loved Him. He gave up everything for the sake of undeserving, sinful, rebellious enemies. We did nothing to earn or deserve His love—yet He loved us nonetheless.

"Though he was rich," Paul says, "yet for your sakes he became poor." What does that mean? In what sense was Jesus "rich"? Was he a billionaire giving away a fortune? No. Paul is not saying Jesus was materially rich—though, as the Creator of the Universe, He certainly was. The wealth of Jesus, God's Son, is measured also in His splendor, His glory, His majesty, His supernatural power, His divine attributes. His wealth is measured in the fact God the Father created all things through Him and for Him.

Above all, His wealth is measured in terms of His eternity. Jesus had no beginning and no end. This verse refutes all of the heretical views about Christ—the claims that Jesus was somehow lower than God, a created being, or a "demigod," or merely a wise human teacher. Jesus had no beginning and no end because He was not a created being. He was and is the Creator God in human form, the Word made flesh.

As Paul wrote elsewhere, "For in Christ all the fullness of the Deity lives in bodily form" (Col. 2:9). Jesus is God over all. He is Jehovah, the Lord of Lords and King of Kings, the omnipotent and omniscient El-Shaddai, "God Almighty." He is the same yesterday, today, and forever. He is the Ruler of the Universe, the object of worship among all the faithful, intelligent creatures in the universe. He is the object of all reverence, love, faith, and devotion.

He claimed equality and oneness with the Father. He said that those who have seen Him have seen the Father. He claimed to have the authority to forgive sins and impart the Holy Spirit to human beings. He claimed to have power to raise you from death to eternal life—and He authenticated His claim by exploding from the tomb in resurrection power.

He gave up all His wealth, power, and eternal splendor for a time so you and I, and all who believe, might become rich—rich in mercy, grace, love, forgiveness, peace, kindness, and eternal life.

Coheirs with Christ

According to *Forbes* magazine, Microsoft founder Bill Gates's net worth in 2006 was approximately $53 billion. What would it mean to you to have your name listed as a beneficiary in Gates's will? If you were to outlive him, you might come into some real money.

But I have good news for you—much better news than

merely being an heir of the Gates estate. The Bible tells us God the Father has written our names into His will—if we have placed our trust in His Son Jesus. As Paul wrote to the Christians in Rome, "The Spirit himself testifies with our spirit that we are God's children. Now if we are children, then we are heirs—heirs of God and co-heirs with Christ, if indeed we share in his sufferings in order that we may also share in his glory" (Rom. 8:16–17).

What does it mean to be an heir of God and a coheir with Christ? What does it mean to have your name appear in the will of the living God? It means you will inherit what Jesus inherits. You will inherit all of His wealth and splendor. That is why we should be generous in our giving. We should give sacrificially and lovingly. We should turn ourselves inside out and empty ourselves when we give. The self-sacrificing, self-emptying love of Jesus should motivate us to give and give and give, joyfully and gratefully.

Martin Luther used to say that to truly become a disciple of Jesus Christ, one has to experience three conversions:

1. a conversion of the heart
2. a conversion of the mind
3. a conversion of the pocketbook.

Most of us readily accept the first two conversions—but we balk at the third. Yet if we take an honest look at the Scriptures, we realize Jesus spoke more about matters of the pocketbook than any other subject, except the Kingdom of God. Why? Because He knew if we would trust Him with our money, our daily needs, our income, and our expenditures, then we would trust Him with anything. But if we can't trust Him for the simple practicalities of life, how can we trust Him with something as vast as eternity?

Today, if you have never done so before, let Jesus have

control of your pocketbook. Let Him have first place in your checkbook, your credit cards, and your ATM cards. Your money bears witness: "In God we trust." May this become more than just a slogan stamped on our money. May it be the transforming truth of our lives.

The Man Who Gave Everything

John Harper was born in 1872 and committed his life to Jesus Christ when he was thirteen years old. From that time forward, John Harper had a passion for sharing the good news of Jesus Christ with everyone he met. By the time he was seventeen, he was walking through the streets of his Scottish village, preaching the gospel and urging people to surrender to the love of God. At age twenty-four, he founded a church near Glasgow, Scotland, with twenty-five members. A dozen years later, there were over five hundred members.

Harper married, but his wife died young, leaving him with a beautiful little daughter to care for. The little girl's name was Nana. In 1911, John Harper came to America and preached a series of evangelistic messages at The Moody Church in Chicago. He was invited back the following year, so on April 10, 1912, he and six-year-old Nana boarded a ship in Southampton, England, and set sail for America. The ship they sailed on was the RMS *Titanic*.

On the night of April 14, the *Titanic* collided with an iceberg in the North Atlantic, opening six watertight compartments to the frigid sea. When it became clear to all on board that the ship was sinking, John Harper put life jackets on himself and his daughter, then took her to the lifeboat. He kissed her and placed her in the arms of a woman in the boat, promising he would see her again someday.

There was room on the lifeboat, and several people urged him to get in with his daughter. He refused. Why? Because there were people on the ship who needed to hear the message of salvation in those last moments before they died. The lifeboat was lowered into the sea without him.

Harper strode up and down the tilting deck, shouting, "Women, children, and unsaved into the lifeboats!" Several times, he was offered a place on a lifeboat, and each time he refused, choosing to stay onboard to preach the message of salvation to those who remained behind.

A horrible roaring noise signaled that the ship was breaking in half. Harper jumped over the rail and into the Atlantic. He found a floating piece of wreckage and clung to it. The salt water was 28 degrees Fahrenheit—colder than the freezing point of freshwater. Floating in those arctic waters was like being encased in ice.

The ocean was dotted with people, some weeping, some moaning, some crying out for help. Harper swam from one to another, sharing the gospel with as many as he could reach, aware that his time was short and hypothermia would soon claim him. He saw one young man clinging to a piece of floating debris. Harper asked him, "Are you saved?" The young man said no—but when Harper tried to share the gospel, the young stranger said bitterly, "Leave me alone!"

Harper wriggled out of his life jacket and gave it to the young man and said, "Take this! You need it more than I do!" Then he swam away to preach to other people. Later, Harper returned—and this time the young man wanted to hear the gospel. Harper shared with him Acts 16:31, "Believe in the Lord Jesus, and you will be saved." The young man believed—and was saved.

Of the more than fifteen hundred people who jumped from the ship into the cold Atlantic that night, only six were rescued. One of them was Harper's young convert. Harper himself was never found. The story of John Harper's last moments was pieced together from survivor accounts.

For years afterward, one *Titanic* survivor traveled around America, speaking in churches and meetings, telling the story of the man who pointed the way to eternal life. "There in the night, with two miles of water beneath me, I believed," the man would say, "I am John Harper's last convert."[1]

Like the One who, though rich, became poor for our sakes, John Harper gave up everything without any thought for himself. He gave up his life and a future with his little daughter. He gave up a place in the lifeboat. He gave up his life jacket. And he gave his last breath for the chance to bring one more soul into the Kingdom.

John Harper gave without thinking of getting. What are you and I willing to give?

Being Appreciated

The nineteenth-century philosopher Thomas Carlyle was born into a strict Christian family, but he lost his Christian faith while studying at the University of Edinburgh. Though he kept the stern, rigid attitudes of his strict upbringing, he lost the love and grace of Christ.

2 Corinthians 9:6–15

While he was young and poor, Carlyle harbored an affection for Kitty Kirkpatrick, a young woman whose father was a British officer and whose mother was a princess of India. The strict class distinctions of that era made it impossible for Carlyle to marry Miss Kirkpatrick, so he took as his bride a kind and beautiful young woman, Jane Welsh. Carlyle couldn't get over his resentment for having to "settle" for marriage to Jane, and he treated her sternly, never giving her any affirmation, appreciation, or affection.

Jane Carlyle couldn't understand what was wrong between them. At her husband's insistence, they slept in separate bedrooms and maintained a hollow, celibate marriage. Jane yearned to be appreciated and she tried to please Thomas, but to no avail. She became depressed and chronically ill, suffering from a number of ailments, including horrible, disabling headaches. She tried to conceal her pain from her husband, always maintaining a cheerful front whenever she was with Thomas, but he was oblivious to her. As her health worsened and her depression deepened, she became a bedridden invalid. After years of illness, Jane died.

After his wife's death, Thomas Carlyle found his wife's diary and began reading. For the first time in his life, he discovered how deeply his wife loved him, and how miserable her life was because of his years of rejection. She wrote about the many times she tried to please him, and how he cruelly rebuffed her. Not once during their marriage had he said a loving or appreciative word to her. He realized she died of a broken heart— and he broke it.

A friend reported finding Carlyle at his wife's grave, weeping and repeating, "If only I had known!" After that, Carlyle withdrew from society and wrote a self-condemning essay, "Reminiscences of Jane Welsh Carlyle."[1]

This tragic story illustrates a deep principle of human nature: we all need to be appreciated. When those who matter to us withhold their appreciation, the spirit within us withers and dies. Sometimes the body dies, too.

The Man Who Gave Everything

The eleventh secret of Paul's fifteen secrets for positive living is: being appreciated. I have never met anyone who does not appreciate being appreciated. Some people will pretend to be totally independent and emotionally self-sufficient: "I'm an island. I don't need anything from anybody. I certainly don't need appreciation from anyone." Don't you believe it. The need to be appreciated is universal.

There are some people who don't know how to express appreciation. Others deliberately withhold appreciation, thinking that such expressions lead people to feel proud or arrogant—but what it usually produces is people who feel rejected, depressed, and starved for attention.

There is nothing wrong with wanting, needing, receiving, or giving appreciation. It is thoroughly biblical and godly to appreciate and be appreciated by one another.

Of course, as in every other area of human activity, there is always the danger of extremes. I once read a story in a Fort Lauderdale, Florida, newspaper about a man who planned his own funeral—then attended his funeral while he was still alive and well. He arrived sitting in the back of a hearse. He sat in the front of the church where he could smell the flowers and hear all the wonderful things that were said about him in the eulogy. He later told the press, "What good does it do for people to say nice things about you after you're dead and can't hear them?"

So if you want to know how much you're appreciated, you can attend your own funeral. But, personally, I'd call that extreme.

Another example of an extreme and unhealthy craving for appreciation is that person who gets completely bent out of shape if others don't "ooh and aah" and gush over every little thing they do. Some people act hurt or angry if they are not continually getting that pat on the back, that word of praise. Clearly, that's not healthy, it's not godly, and it's not biblical. It's extreme.

I'm not suggesting we should go to extremes. I'm only suggesting what Paul advocates—we should express normal biblical appreciation toward one another.

An anonymous poet penned some lines entitled "One Little Rose." It reads:

> I would rather have one little rose
> From the garden of a friend
> Than to have the choicest flowers
> When my stay on earth must end.
> I would rather have a pleasant word
> In kindness said to me
> Than flattery when my heart is still,
> And life has ceased to be.
>
> I would rather have a loving smile
> From friends I know are true
> Than tears shed 'round my casket
> When to this world I bid adieu.
>
> Bring me all your flowers today,
> Whether pink, or white, or red;
> I'd rather have one blossom now
> Than a truckload when I'm dead.[2]

The Scriptures recognize the need to give and receive appreciation is normal and universal. Paul writes, "Give everyone what you owe him: If you owe . . . respect, then respect; if honor, then honor" (Rom. 13:7). Paul also wrote, "So speak encouraging words to one another. Build up hope so you'll all be together in this, no one left out, no one left behind. I know you're already doing this; just keep on doing it. And now, friends, we ask you to honor those leaders who work so hard for you, who have been given the responsibility of urging and guiding you along in your obedience. Overwhelm them with appreciation and love!" (1 Thess. 5:11-12, THE MESSAGE).

A Danish philosopher once said, "Ingratitude is always a form of weakness. I have never known a truly strong person to be ungrateful." By this definition, God is the strongest Person of all. Why? Because, though He needs nothing from us, He lavishes appreciation upon us. Throughout the Scriptures, we see that God does not let even one small act of sacrifice or effort on our part go unappreciated or unrewarded.

Imagine if God blessed you with a million dollars. You put the money in your bank account—and then you saw Joe the Street Preacher needed a car in order to continue his ministry in the city streets. So you took out your checkbook and you wrote a check for $20,000 and bought Joe the Street Preacher a nice late-model car. You could have gotten him something older and more beat-up, but you wanted him to have a dependable car for his ministry, so you bought him the $20,000 car.

Next imagine that God comes to you and says, "That was a wonderful thing you did for Joe the Street Preacher. Thank you so much. That car is going to be a big help to his ministry. I applaud you. Well done."

How would you respond? You might say, "I don't deserve any thanks. After all, I was only able to write that check, Lord, because You blessed me with a million dollars. Compared to what You gave me, I only gave a pittance. How can You thank me and reward me when You have given me so much?"

Yet that is how God shows His appreciation for us all the time. He has blessed us with so much—yet every time we do some paltry little act of kindness to someone else, He appreciates it. He rewards us. He pats us on the back. We are only sharing a tiny portion of our blessings with others—yet God showers us with appreciation. That's His nature. His fatherly appreciation of our baby steps of generosity are yet another sign of His overwhelming grace toward us.

Sowing and Reaping

In the previous passage, we saw that Paul's tenth secret for positive living is: getting through giving. In this next passage, Paul tells us God appreciates and rewards generous givers. He writes: "Remember this: Whoever sows sparingly will also reap sparingly, and whoever sows generously will also reap generously" (2 Cor. 9:6).

Are you a farmer? Or a gardener? Did you at least study a little plant biology in school? Good. Because in this verse, Paul makes an analogy involving planting seeds and growing crops. He was speaking to an agrarian society, and in that society, people had no trouble grasping the meaning of his analogy.

Paul is saying that if you scatter an abundance of seeds on the ground, you will get an abundant crop. That's only reasonable. And if you are stingy with your seed and you scatter it sparsely on the ground, then you will get a stingy, sparse, anemic crop. That, too, is only reasonable.

There is a story told in the Orient that makes a similar point. One day, a group of potato farmers decided they would sort their potatoes, reserving the largest ones for their dinner tables while saving the smallest ones for seed. After several years of this practice, they noticed that each year the harvest produced smaller and smaller potatoes. Why? Because they were, in effect, *breeding* small potatoes by only *planting* small potatoes. The result was they were harvesting smaller potatoes—out of which they would select the smallest for planting. They realized that to continue this practice would ultimately result in a harvest of marble-sized potatoes.

They learned the lesson Paul teaches us here: Whoever plants sparingly will also reap sparingly, and whoever plants generously will also reap generously. The harvest is in direct proportion to the sowing of the seed.

Paul then tells us God's depth of appreciation for us is in

proportion to our spirit of generosity in giving back to God.
His blessings will unfold in our lives as we practice the principle of generous giving. God expresses His appreciation and
blessing toward us, His children, in four ways:

1. God will have a "soft spot" in His heart for us (verse 7).
2. God will provide abundantly for all our needs (verses
   8–11).
3. God will be glorified through us (verses 11–13).
4. God will answer prayers offered on our behalf (verses
   14–15).

Let's look at each of these four ways God shows His appreciation for our generosity in giving back to Him.

Blessing Number 1: A "Soft Spot" in God's Heart

God is looking for a lifestyle of what Paul literally calls "hilarious" giving. He writes, "Each man should give what he has
decided in his heart to give, not reluctantly or under compulsion, for God loves a cheerful giver" (2 Cor. 9:7).

In the original New Testament Greek language, the word
translated "cheerful" ("God loves a cheerful giver") is *"hilaros"*—the word from which we get our English word "hilarious." The Greek word *"hilaros"* has a much stronger meaning
than simply "cheerful." It suggests someone who is eager to
give, who feels joyous giving. Giving makes a *hilaros* giver
merry. Such a giver actually has *fun* writing a check to God—it
makes him laughing-out-loud jolly. That's the kind of giver God
loves to see. In fact, God has a "soft spot" in His vast heart for
cheerful, hilarious givers.

Paul also tells us, "Each man should give what he has decided in his heart to give, not reluctantly or under compulsion."
We see a lot of that kind of giving in the Christian world today,

where people are compelled to give by means appealing to guilt or tugging at their emotions or using slick, manipulative pressure techniques. Paul says God wants nothing to do with money extorted from people by trickery and manipulation. We in the church should never try to compel or shame people into giving. God wants churches full of cheerful, hilarious, intentional givers—not a bunch of reluctant sheep to be sheared and fleeced.

Who are the cheerful givers? Those whose giving to God comes from a grateful heart, not a reluctant sense of obligation. Those whose giving to God is joyful and continual and systematic. Those whose giving to God is intentional and voluntary, not compelled or manipulated.

Notice again Paul's promise to believers who give from a heart full of hilarious love and gratitude toward the Father: "God loves a cheerful giver." That is a wonderful promise. This is God's promise that a cheerful, merry, hilarious giver will have a special place in the affections of the Creator God.

Now, we all know God loves everybody in a general sense. He loves the saints and the sinners, the virgins and the prostitutes, the peacemakers and the terrorists. God's universal love for humanity is what Jesus spoke of when He said, "For God so loved the world that he gave his one and only Son, that whoever believes in him shall not perish but have eternal life" (John 3:16).

Yet, God also has a special love for His own, a love Jesus described when he said that "the Father himself loves you because you have loved me and have believed that I came from God" (John 16:27). God has a general love for all humanity, but He has a focused and responsive love for those individuals who love Jesus the Son and believe in Him. God also has a special, responsive love, as Paul describes, for those who give to God, freely and cheerfully, from a heart full of love and gratitude. He has reserved a "soft spot" in His heart for those who choose to give generously back to Him a portion of what He has graciously showered upon us all.

I think we all like to be appreciated, but there are some people in our lives whose expressions of appreciation are more meaningful than others. Appreciation from someone who matters deeply to us—a spouse, a parent, a child—means more to us than a perfunctory "thank you" from a stranger.

So imagine what it truly means to you that the God who created heaven and earth expresses His appreciation to you. Imagine what it means that there is a "soft spot" in His heart for you. There can be no sweeter and more uplifting thought. Almighty God appreciates *you* because you have given willingly, eagerly, cheerfully, to Him.

Blessing Number 2: God Will Provide Abundantly for All Our Needs

God shows His appreciation to generous, cheerful givers by providing abundantly for their every need. Paul writes:

> And God is able to make all grace abound to you, so that in all things at all times, having all that you need, you will abound in every good work. As it is written:
>   "He has scattered abroad his gifts to the poor;
>   his righteousness endures forever."
> Now he who supplies seed to the sower and bread for food will also supply and increase your store of seed and will enlarge the harvest of your righteousness. You will be made rich in every way so that you can be generous on every occasion, and through us your generosity will result in thanksgiving to God.

> *(2 Corinthians 9:8–11)*

We all know it is possible to give without loving. You can give in order to receive a payback, a kickback, a quid pro quo. You can give in order to get a tax deduction. You can give in order to make yourself look important and generous. You can give for all kinds of reasons that have nothing to do with love, but you cannot love without giving.

If you claim to love, but you do not express your love in giving, then you do not truly love. God showed His love to us by giving His Son and by showering us with blessings far beyond our deserving. So we must ask ourselves: "If we say we *love* God, but we do not *give* to God, do we *truly* love Him? Where is the proof of our love?"

Because God has a special love for those who love His Son, for those who are cheerful givers, He "is able to make all grace abound to you, so that in all things at all times, having all that you need, you will abound in every good work." God's gracious giving is limitless, it's measureless, it's off the chart.

Why does God appreciate our giving so much? It's because He knows our giving is proof of our faith in Him and our trust in Him. The way we give to God is a tangible demonstration of our level of faith. It shows whether we are living by faith—or by sight.

If you give to God out of a heart that lacks faith, then your natural human perception, the eyes of sight, will say, "What are you doing? You're squandering your resources. You're endangering your net worth and your financial security on earth. You'll have less money left over if you give to God. You may need that money. How do you know God will continue to supply your needs? If you give that money to God, you'll be sorry." That's the world's view of giving. That's what giving looks like through the eyes of natural human perception.

But the eyes of faith say, "No, no! That's not the case at all! When I give to God, I'll have more, not less. I'm investing God's resources, and building my net worth in heaven. I'm storing up treasures in heaven that can never be taken away. If I give to God, I'll have *more* left over, not less, because I can always trust God to take care of my needs. God loves a cheerful giver and He always shows His appreciation to those He loves."

God appreciates it when we walk by faith and not by sight. It thrills the heart of God to see us living in the world of faith instead of the world of sight. He loves to see us stepping out in faith and trusting in His promises instead of trusting human wisdom by holding on to our worldly wealth. God deeply appreciates those who live as though all things are possible, and there is nothing too hard for God. If you have never experienced God's appreciation to you for boldly living the adventure of faith, then you are missing out on the greatest joy you can ever experience.

I have seen this principle at work again and again, in my own life and in the lives of my family: God replenishes what we give so we never lack for any good thing.

Suppose I have two five-dollar bills—that's all I have in the world. So I go to God and pray, "Lord, You've blessed me. I'm overwhelmed with my blessings." And I count up all my blessings—my family, my church, my health, and on and on. In conclusion, I say, "Lord, in gratitude for all of these blessings, I'm going to give one of these five-dollar bills to You."

Now, if I were not a cheerful giver, but a reluctant and grudging giver, I would "come to my senses" after giving God that five-dollar bill, and I'd say, "What was I thinking? What did I do *that* for? Now I've only got five dollars left. I could have had ten. What a fool I was. I should have kept it."

The cheerful giver is hilarious with joy. He says, "God, thank You that I have the privilege of giving that five dollars to You. Thank You for the joy of giving! What a great God You are! I may only have five dollars to my name right now, but I know You're going to stretch that five dollars and it's going to go around the block a few times. Nothing's impossible for You. Thank You, Lord!"

And you know what will happen if you are a cheerful, hilarious giver? The very thing you need most will arrive from a completely unexpected source. And you'll say, "Bless the Lord, more money to give to God!" And as you keep thanking God and giving back to Him, you'll find money and resources popping up here and there, all over the place.

That's the world of faith. That's the realm where "impossible" things happen all the time because nothing is impossible for God. It overwhelms me to see God at work this way, but it is absolutely, reliably, and consistently true. He provides all the grace, all the resources, all the time, all the sufficiency we need. This is not theory for me. This is a proven fact. And I can't wait to see the gifts of God's grace and appreciation He will lavish upon us as we enjoy eternity with Him.

Back in 1978, when I was a seminary student in California, God began to teach me these lessons in a very personal way. In those days, I was struggling financially, and I would rationalize about giving to God. I'd say, "God, You know I don't have much to give. You called me to be a minister of the gospel and I've given myself to You. I've given everything to You, Lord. And You know, if I was out in the world, I'd be making five times as much money as I'm making in the ministry; so in a way, I'm really giving to You out of all the money I would have made if I was in some other profession."

Now, you can see how foolish that rationalization was—but I tried to sell that idea to God. And every time I'd make that argument to God, I sensed Him saying to me, "Michael, stop being ridiculous. You can't argue with me. You've got to put the cash in there."

So God worked on me to teach me this lesson. I will never forget the day in 1978, while I was still in school in California,

I had fifty-five dollars in my account. I had nothing I could sell or pawn to raise some cash, not even a decent watch. Based on my income, my tithe was fifty dollars. If I gave the whole fifty dollars to the Lord, I'd be left with five dollars, period. But God was working on my heart, and I knew what He wanted me to do.

So I wrote a check for fifty dollars, put it in an envelope, walked it over to the mailbox, and dropped it in. Then I went over to my post office box to pick up my mail. It was less than a two-minute walk from the mailbox to my post office box. I opened my box, took out my mail, and there was an envelope that was thicker than the average letter. I opened the envelope and took out . . .

Cash! The envelope was stuffed with hundred-dollar bills— a total of $1,300! It's foolish to mail that much money in cash, but there it was.

I checked the note that was enclosed with the money and found it was from a couple I knew. I officiated at their wedding some weeks earlier. They gave me a small gift at the time, and I thought, *Well, that's a nice gift*, and I never gave it another thought. Now, out of the blue, they sent me $1,300 in cash.

The note said, "To those who are superstitious, number thirteen is bad luck. But to my wife and me, the number thirteen has always meant blessing. That envelope contained thirteen $100 bills. God has blessed us many times by means of the number thirteen." God used that experience to encourage my small faith.

Human wisdom says prosperity comes from accumulating and hoarding. Human wisdom says, "Get all you can, can all you get, and sit on the lid." But faith says, "God's promises are true, they can be trusted. God loves and appreciates a cheerful giver. A cheerful giver will be made rich in every way so his cheerful generosity results in thanksgiving to God."

Blessing Number 3: God Will Be Glorified Through Us

When other people are blessed by our generosity, they will give praise and glory to God. They will give credit to the Lord—but He will give credit to us for our intentional, voluntary, cheerful generosity. Paul writes, "This service that you perform is not only supplying the needs of God's people but is also overflowing in many expressions of thanks to God. Because of the service by which you have proved yourselves, men will praise God for the obedience that accompanies your confession of the gospel of Christ, and for your generosity in sharing with them and with everyone else" (2 Cor. 9:12-13).

If you look around at the society in which we live, you have to conclude that most people today are like spoiled brats who have received everything and are thankful for nothing. We have so much wealth and prosperity, free education, quality health care, guaranteed rights and freedoms, opportunities for employment and self-employment, and on and on. Yet many of the people who enjoy all of these things seem to feel entitled to it all. There is no gratitude, no appreciation of God's grace in their lives.

This attitude of ingratitude, which is so pervasive in our society, grieves the heart of God. But in these verses, Paul tells us our acts of service toward unbelievers will break through that barrier of entitlement and ingratitude, and "men will praise God for the obedience that accompanies your confession of the gospel of Christ."

Paul goes on to make another point in these verses we should be careful not to miss. He writes, "*Because of the service by which you have proved yourselves*, men will praise God for the obedience that accompanies your confession of the gospel of Christ." Paul is saying that we, as Christians, go about testifying to the gospel of Jesus Christ—but how do the unsaved people around us know that our gospel is true? What evidence do they have for believing our gospel?

The proof is right here: *"Because of the service by which you have proved yourselves."* When we provide tangible evidence that Jesus Christ lives within us through our cheerful generosity, we prove we belong to Him, and He is real in our lives. Our service and generosity is *proof* that God lives, Jesus is Lord, and our salvation is the real deal.

Genuine Christianity is proved by generous giving. Genuine salvation is expressed in generous obedience. Our obedience always brings glory to God.

At this point, let's look at the background of this letter. In the previous letter, in 1 Corinthians 16, we see the Gentile Christians in Corinth have taken up a collection for the poverty-stricken Jewish Christians in Jerusalem. Not only were the saints in Jerusalem suffering persecution for their faith, but they were also suffering the effects of an area-wide famine. So the church in Jerusalem was reduced to poverty. Now it was the privilege of the Gentile churches, including the church in Corinth, to contribute to the needs of the suffering believers in Jerusalem.

The poverty-stricken saints in Jerusalem knew of the city of Corinth only by its reputation. The city of Corinth was known throughout the Roman Empire as a city of immorality and idolatry. It was the "Sin City" of its day. Every vice and forbidden pleasure known to man was available in Corinth.

So imagine the incredible joy of the believers in Jerusalem when they heard there was a powerful witness, a strong Christian fellowship, in the city of Corinth. Even more wonderful, these Gentile believers were standing with the Jerusalem believers and supporting them in their hour of need. The Jerusalem Christians must have said, "Wow! Glory to God! He has called people out of that 'Sin City' to be our brothers and sisters in Christ. May God be praised!"

So Paul said to the Corinthians, "This service that you perform is not only supplying the needs of God's people but is also overflowing in many expressions of thanks to God."

Blessing Number 4: God Will Answer Prayers Offered on Our Behalf

The fourth way God expresses His appreciation and blessing toward us when we give cheerfully to Him is He answers prayers offered on our behalf. Paul writes, "And in their prayers for you their hearts will go out to you, because of the surpassing grace God has given you. Thanks be to God for his indescribable gift!" (2 Cor. 9:14–15).

On one occasion, I was overseas, recording thirty radio messages in three days. My interpreter, Rev. Baki Sadaka, was in the studio and we were in the middle of recording when we had a technical problem and had to wait for the problem to be fixed. While we were waiting, Baki said to me, "Did you know, brother, that there are believers all around the world who pray for The Church of The Apostles on a daily basis? Every day at seven-thirty in the morning, The Church of The Apostles is aired in one hundred ninety-one countries around the world. And wherever I go, people say to me, 'We watch the telecast every day before we go to work and then we give thanks to God for The Church of The Apostles.'"

My heart was touched to realize so many believers in poverty-stricken parts of the world are praying for our church in America. I'm reminded of how the poor believers in famine-plagued Jerusalem prayed for the church in rich, sin-plagued Corinth. Sometimes we who are rich here in the West are tempted to think, *What can a poor believer do for me? I'm rich and he is poor.*

But Paul said the prayers of the poor in Jerusalem are the very blessing the rich Corinthians would receive back from the

Lord. "In their prayers for you," Paul said, "their hearts will go out to you, because of the surpassing grace God has given you. Thanks be to God for his indescribable gift!"

Dr. Helen Roseveare is a retired Christian missionary from England who served in the Congo, in central Africa, from 1953 to 1973. During the violent uprisings of the 1960s, when many missionaries left the Congo, Helen Roseveare remained to minister among the people she loved. In 1964, she was captured by rebel forces and held prisoner for five months. During that time, she was repeatedly beaten, raped, and threatened with death.

Finally, the rebels released her without any explanation. She returned to England for more than a year for medical treatment and recuperation. Then she courageously went back to the Congo to help establish a new hospital and medical school after the previous one (which she also helped establish) was destroyed. Since her retirement in 1973, she has lived in Northern Ireland. Her story was portrayed in the film *Mama Luka Comes Home* (1989).

Dr. Roseveare tells a story of answered prayer. "A mother at our mission station died after giving birth to a premature baby," she recalls. "We tried to improvise an incubator to keep the infant alive, but the only hot water bottle we had was worn beyond repair. So we asked the children to pray for the orphaned baby and her sister. One of the girls prayed, 'Dear God, please send a hot water bottle today. Tomorrow will be too late because by then the baby will be dead. And dear Lord, send a doll for the baby's sister so she won't feel so lonely without her mother.'

"That very afternoon, a large package arrived from England. The children watched eagerly as we opened it. Much to their surprise, under some clothing was a hot water bottle! Immediately, the girl who had prayed so earnestly started to dig deeper, exclaiming, 'If God sent a hot water bottle, I'm sure He also sent a doll!'

"And she was right! There was a doll underneath the hot water bottle. The Heavenly Father knew in advance of that child's sincere requests. Five months before that prayer was even prayed, God led a ladies' group to include both of the specific articles the girl had prayed for."

Truly, we serve a God of surpassing grace and awesome appreciation. His generosity is infinite—and He rewards every one of our faltering attempts to imitate His generosity.

Thanks be to God for His indescribable gift!

When Pride Is Good

General John Sedgwick was in the Union Army during the American Civil War. He was a close friend of officers on both sides of the war, including General Robert E. Lee, the commander of the Confederate forces, and General Ulysses S. Grant, commander of the Union forces. On May 9, 1864, General Sedgwick commanded a corps in the Battle of Spotsylvania Court House in central Virginia. After sending units out along the skirmish lines to test the Confederate defenses, he was directing the placement of artillery units in an open field.

2 Corinthians 10:1–18

Suddenly, shots rang out from a distant tree line, about a thousand yards away. Rebel sharpshooters were sniping at the Union troops as they set up the artillery pieces. The Union artillery men scattered, but Sedgwick stood proud and tall in the middle of the open field, shouting to his men, "What are you doing? Fleeing for cover because of a few stray bullets? You men should be ashamed! Those Rebs couldn't hit an elephant at this distance!"

Those were General Sedgwick's last words. The very next instant, he dropped to the ground, struck instantly dead by a Confederate bullet. "Pride goes before destruction," warns Proverbs 16:18, "a haughty spirit before a fall." General Sedgwick was literally—and fatally—felled by his own pride.

The Symptoms of Pride

You've heard of the seven deadly sins—pride, greed, envy, wrath, lust, gluttony, and sloth. Pride always tops the list of those seven sins. It is, after all, the sin by which the angels fell. The word "pride" is variously defined as *an unduly elevated opinion of oneself* or *an arrogant assumption of one's own superiority*. However you define it, the sin of pride involves being absorbed with oneself. As someone has observed, it is fitting that the letter *I* is in the center of the word "pride."

The sin of pride is better understood in terms of its symptoms than in terms of a dictionary definition. The symptoms of sinful pride include:

- stealing from God's glory and taking credit for the gifts He has given us
- self-centeredness
- stubborn and self-willed spirit
- attitude of superiority
- sarcasm and insensitivity to the feelings of others
- judgmental and critical attitude
- impatience toward other people
- unteachable spirit (resistance to instruction; an unwillingness to learn from other people)

- self-pity (an unhealthy absorption in one's own problems; feeling one's troubles are totally unfair and far worse than everyone else's)
- shifting blame to others; refusing to take responsibility for one's own mistakes and choices.

Each of us, at one point or another in our lives, exhibits some or all of these symptoms of unhealthy pride. So how do we gain the victory over pride? There is only one proven cure for sinful, unhealthy pride: every day, express your utter dependence upon God in all areas of your life.

There is nothing you have, and nothing you are, for which you can claim credit. If you are attractive and talented, thank God for the genes with which He blessed you. Are you more intelligent than average? You probably had some educational advantages and parents who encouraged your mental development. Do you take credit for all the hard work you do that made you so successful? Well, who taught you the value of hard work? Who gave you a healthy body and a good mind so you could reap the rewards of your labor? Who decided you would be born into a land of limitless opportunity for success? You might just as easily have been one of the billions born in situations of poverty and starvation.

When we start to count all the blessings we have received from the hand of God, of what do we have to be so proud? We are utterly dependent upon God for all we have and all we are. This is true of our professional life, our personal life—and, most of all, our spiritual life. After all, we did not choose God; He reached down to us. We were dead in our sins, incapable of saving ourselves—but God in His grace sent Jesus to die for us. If that immense truth doesn't vanquish all of our foolish pride, what will?

Dr. Peter Marshall was born in Scotland and arrived in America as a penniless immigrant in 1927. He worked his way through

Columbia Theological Seminary and rose to become one of the leading pastors in America and chaplain of the United States Senate. Despite his accomplishments, everyone who knew him remarked that he was an amazingly humble man. Peter Marshall's advice about the sin of pride was simply this: "When successful . . . don't crow. When defeated . . . don't croak."

A Pride You Can Be Proud Of!

Have you ever struggled with the sin of pride? Millions of Christians do. I have struggled with pride myself. But I want to show you how, starting today, you can channel this struggle. I'm going to tell you about something I call "good pride," a pride you can cultivate and practice with a clear conscience. Indeed, it's a pride you can truly be proud of!

This is the twelfth of the fifteen secrets of positive living—the principle I call: when pride is good. Is there truly such a thing as "good pride"? Absolutely! In fact, the apostle Paul, in this next passage, describes a kind of pride so good you could even call it "holy pride" or "godly pride." Paul writes: "But, 'Let him who boasts boast in the Lord.' For it is not the one who commends himself who is approved, but the one whom the Lord commends" (2 Cor. 10:17–18).

In fact, the entire tenth chapter of 2 Corinthians deals with the characteristics of "good pride." You can display this kind of pride to your heart's content. You can brag this kind of pride without any concern that you might be sinning. You can enjoy this kind of pride without guilt. You can revel in it, delight in it, and live in it every day of your life.

"Let him who boasts boast in the Lord." If you want to brag about anything, then brag all you want about God and His goodness. As we shall see in the rest of this passage, Paul outlines for us three characteristics of this form of godly boasting, this holy pride:

1. "Good pride" shows mercy.
2. "Good pride" builds up.
3. "Good pride" is tenacious.

Let's look at each of these characteristics in turn.

1. "Good Pride" Shows Mercy

The difference between good pride and sinful pride is clear: Sinful pride is self-seeking. When wounded, sinful pride strikes back. When insulted, sinful pride turns nasty and vengeful. When injured, sinful pride shows no mercy.

But godly pride is gentle, patient, and gracious. In the first verse of this passage, Paul writes, "By the meekness and gentleness of Christ, I appeal to you—"

What is "meekness"? Many people confuse meekness with weakness. If you look up the word in an English dictionary, you'll find a definition much like this one: *docile, tame, without spirit, or overly submissive*. Does that sound like the Jesus you know? Even when Jesus allowed Himself to be arrested in the Garden of Gethsemane, tried before Pontius Pilate, and nailed to a Roman cross, He was far from "docile, tame, without spirit, or overly submissive."

The soldiers and religious officials, armed with weapons, came to the garden to arrest Jesus—and He boldly went out to meet them. "Who is it you want?" he asked. "Jesus of Nazareth," they replied. Jesus said, "I am he." Those three words caused the startled men to fall backward to the ground. Their torches and swords were no match for the mere sound of His voice. He was meek—yet His enemies couldn't even stand upright in the presence of his strong, bold personality (see John 18).

If the very meekness of Jesus is that powerful, then this word "meekness" clearly cannot mean *weakness*. It *must* have some other meaning. In fact, the original Greek word translated as "meekness" is *"praiotes."* This word does not mean *weakness*. In fact, there is no one word in English that quite conveys the rich meaning of the original Greek word. It has a meaning which suggests *power that is used with gentleness and humility; strength under control.*

Meekness is *strength*—under control.

Genuine Christlike meekness is displayed when you have the upper hand, the ability to hurt your opponent, to destroy your enemy—but you choose not to. Meekness is when you are in a position of strength and power—yet you choose not to use that power against your opponent, your critic, your accuser, your persecutor.

You might say, "Michael, that's unrealistic. This idea of meekness could never work in the real world. It could never work in my day-to-day life. Michael, I didn't make the rules—I just live by them. And the number one rule in the real world is: 'Do one to others before they do one to you.' It's a dog-eat-dog world out there. You've got to eat the other dog before he sinks his fangs into you."

My friend, do you really think times are tougher for you in the twenty-first century than they were for Jesus and Paul in the first century? The people of that time questioned the sanity and practicality of Christlike meekness just as much as people do today. If you want to know what a "dog-eat-dog" world *really* looks like, read up on life in the Roman Empire of Paul's day. Yet, Paul insists, as Christians, we are to live by the meekness and gentleness of Christ.

The people of Paul's day saw his meekness as weakness. They misinterpreted Paul's mercy and compassion as a lack of confidence. They mistook his "power under control" for "no power at all." Christlike meekness and humility are qualities the world has never understood—and never will. The world doesn't understand how we can speak boldly for the truth—yet show compassion and humility toward our opponents. They hear us speaking out boldly for Christ and for Christian values and morality, and they say, "How arrogant those Christians are. How judgmental they are. How intolerant they are. How bigoted."

The world cannot understand how Christians can speak out against abortion and sexual promiscuity and permissiveness—yet show compassion and nonjudgmental caring toward women and girls with crisis pregnancies. The world cannot understand how Christians can say homosexual activity and drug abuse are sins—yet show compassion and caring toward people with AIDS and addictions.

The world cannot understand how Christians can hate the sin and love the sinner—but that is what true Christlike meekness is all about. Jesus continually confronted sin—yet He always comforted and accepted sinners. Now He calls us to follow His example of grace and truth, His example of meekness.

A person who boasts in the Lord truly has a "humble pride," a pride that is focused on God, not on the self. It has been said that a humble person doesn't think less of himself; he just thinks of himself less. He has a genuine understanding and conviction that he is totally unworthy of the grace of God. He gives God all the credit for the good things in his life.

Paul exemplified "humble pride." He said he was nothing but a clay pot, a wretched man, the least of all saints, the last of the apostles, and the foremost of sinners. What a contrast he was to the self-seeking pride and arrogance of his opponents, the false teachers. Paul is saying to us that we are to take pride in who God is. That is a good, holy pride. We are to be boldly proud and outspoken on behalf of biblical truth—and we must do so with Christlike meekness and compassion.

Was Jesus a "wimp" because He allowed Himself to be tortured and crucified? No! His willingness to submit to the cross made Him the strongest man who ever lived. He had the power to step down from the cross, destroy His tormentors, and condemn the world to hell—but in His awesome love and magnificent meekness, He chose to suffer and die for our sakes.

Was Paul a "wimp" because he dealt compassionately and patiently with the Corinthians when he was among them? Hardly. However, some of Paul's opponents actually called him "timid." His reply to his critics in Corinth was: "By the meekness and gentleness of Christ, I appeal to you—I, Paul, who am 'timid' when face to face with you, but 'bold' when away! . . . I do not want to seem to be trying to frighten you with my letters. For some say, 'His letters are weighty and forceful, but in person he is unimpressive and his speaking amounts to nothing.' Such people should realize that what we are in our letters when we are absent, we will be in our actions when we are present" (2 Cor. 10:1, 9–11).

Can you imagine anyone calling Paul "timid"? This man's courage speaks for itself. He faced angry mobs, suffered multiple beatings, stonings, floggings, false imprisonment, and shipwrecks. He looked powerful King Agrippa in the eye and told him to repent or face the judgment of God. What foolishness it was to call this courageous man "timid"—to call him a "wimp!"

So, in a few concise sentences, Paul set the record straight. The carping of his critics didn't bother Paul. He simply wanted to make sure his true friends in Corinth didn't believe the lies of the false apostles.

Paul knew his strength didn't come from his physical toughness—though he was able to endure more suffering and punishment than a dozen other human beings. Paul knew his strength didn't come from his intellect—though he was certainly a brilliant scholar and debater, an intellectual powerhouse. Paul knew his strength didn't come from his speaking ability—though he possessed an unparalleled ability to articulate God's truth.

Paul took no pride in any of his many human strengths and

abilities. He took no pride in who he was or what he could do. But Paul was a man of boastful pride when it came to this one truth: "Let him who boasts boast in the Lord."

Boasting in the Lord means we put our confidence in Him, not in weapons of argument, ability, intellect, or physical force. That's why Paul says, "For though we live in the world, we do not wage war as the world does. The weapons we fight with are not the weapons of the world. On the contrary, they have divine power to demolish strongholds. We demolish arguments and every pretension that sets itself up against the knowledge of God, and we take captive every thought to make it obedient to Christ" (2 Cor. 10:3-5).

Have you heard of the branch of theology called "apologetics"? It may sound like it's the science of saying, "I'm sorry," but apologetics actually deals with intellectually proving or defending the Christian faith. It is a valid and important area of study. The apostle Peter said, "Always be prepared to give an answer to everyone who asks you to give the reason for the hope that you have. But do this with gentleness and respect" (1 Pet. 3:15b). (Note, by the way, that Peter's word "gentleness" (*"prautes"* in Greek) is a form of the word Paul uses for "meekness."

Today, we see many Christian apologists vigorously defending the faith and arguing proofs for Christianity. They are stirring up controversies and making headlines—but are they leading many people to Christ? It doesn't appear so. Why is that? Perhaps it is because these apologists rely on their intellect, their eloquence, their knowledge, and their debating ability.

Paul said we must not wage war as the world does. Instead, we are to use weapons of divine power, which are able to demolish arguments and strongholds. We boast only in the Lord—and we do so in meekness, gentleness, and with courteous respect toward our opponents. Our goal is not to destroy those who oppose us, but to love them into the Kingdom. The weapons of God's power, unleashed through prayer, can demolish human foolishness, destroy Satan's lies, and put our enemy to flight—and they can win over our enemies, converting them into brothers and sisters in Christ.

Paul understood divine power better than anyone. On the road to Damascus, he was impacted by that power, blinded by it, and transformed by it. This former Pharisee and persecutor of Christians had once been an unassailable fortress of human pride and religious knowledge. No intellectual arguments could have swayed him or convinced him Jesus truly was the Christ and the risen Lord. Only divine power could tear down the fortress walls of the preconversion Paul.

The power of the Word of God coupled with the power of prayer can destroy every argument and tear down every stronghold. Nothing can stand against the power of God, the power that spoke time and space into existence. And that power can only be wielded through meekness and gentleness, not through force, intimidation, argument, and intellectual brilliance. The power of God is divine strength under divine control, made available through prayer to mere mortals like you and me.

Good pride doesn't seek to vanquish and destroy enemies; it wins enemies over. Good pride doesn't attack; it persuades. Good pride shows mercy—even to opponents.

2. "Good Pride" Builds Up

Paul pleads with the Corinthians to examine the evidence objectively. He writes: "You are looking only on the surface of things. If anyone is confident that he belongs to Christ, he should consider again that we belong to Christ just as much as he. For even if I boast somewhat freely about the authority the Lord gave us for building you up rather than pulling you down, I will not be ashamed of it. I do not want to seem to be trying to frighten you with my letters. For some say, 'His letters are weighty and forceful, but in person he is unimpressive and his speaking amounts to nothing.' Such people should realize that what we are in our letters when we are absent, we will be in our actions when we are present" (2 Cor. 10:7-11).

In other words, Paul says, "Do not judge me by appearances. Look at how I have lived my life. Ask my colleagues who travel with me day and night. Don't be taken in by the outward appearance of false teachers. Examine their life and compare it with mine."

Just as in Paul's day, there are prideful false teachers who seek to tear down the lives and reputations of God's servants. Sinful pride tears people down. Godly pride—the kind of pride that boasts only in the Lord—builds people up. Whenever we hear rumors and gossip being spread about God's servants, we should ask ourselves:

• Does the person spreading this information live a life that impacts people in a positive way—or a negative way? In the past, has this person edified and built up the church—or torn it down with conflict and division? Does this person strengthen the ministry of the church—or weaken it? Does this person help people grow spiritually—or hinder them?

• And what about the victim of the rumor? In the past, has this Christian servant impacted people positively—or negatively? Has this servant of Christ edified and built up the church—or torn it down with conflict and division? Strengthen the ministry of the church—or weaken it? Help people grow spiritually—or hinder them? If this person has always led an exemplary life before, does it make sense to believe the worst about this person now? Could the rumor be a lie?

You'll often find those who carry rumors and harm the reputations of God's servants are like those false teachers who

attacked Paul. They tend to have a track record of destruction. They have left a trail of human misery, divided churches,
rumors, conflict, ministries harmed or destroyed, and people
they've hurt who have left the church and left the faith. The tar-
gets of their rumors and whispering campaigns are usually the
ones God is using in a strategic way to advance His Kingdom.

So look at the track record—and that will tell you who to believe and who to ignore. We are to judge not according to who
looks good, who gives the most glib and persuasive speech,
who plays a convincing role. We are to judge according to their
actions and the results we see in their lives.

"Good pride" boasts in the Lord, and "good pride" builds
up. In light of this principle, consider this: Theological liberals
and apostate Christians seldom build good institutions. They
tear down what has been established. This has been the case
since the founding of the Christian faith.

Orthodox Christians have consistently maintained and preserved the beliefs, doctrines, and traditions that were first entrusted to the church by Jesus and the apostles—beliefs and
traditions such as the virgin birth of Christ, the atoning death
of Christ, the literal bodily resurrection of Christ, and the truth
that Jesus is the way, the truth, and the life. As Peter said, "Salvation is found in no one else, for there is no other name under
heaven given to men by which we must be saved" (Acts 4:12).

Read the statements and publications of liberal and apostate
theologians. They always hijack Christian tradition while denying Christian truth. They tear down the structure of truths and
doctrines Jesus Himself set forth and godly people have carefully preserved over the centuries. In my former denomination,
there is a famous bishop, now retired, who has written a book
called *A New Christianity for a New World*. What would this
bishop's "new Christianity" look like if it were to replace the
Christianity we all know?

Well, this "new Christianity" would have no actual living

God who is real and involved in human affairs. "God" would be reduced to a symbol or idea. On his Web site, this man writes, "Theism, as a way of defining God, is dead. So most theological God-talk is today meaningless. A new way to speak of God must be found." This "new Christianity" would also have no Christ. He writes, "Since God can no longer be conceived in theistic terms, it becomes nonsensical to seek to understand Jesus as the incarnation of the theistic deity." So in just a few sentences, this bishop has torn down the very foundation of Christianity—the existence of God and the identity of Christ.

This liberal theologian goes on to disparage the biblical story of the Creation and the Fall of Man as "pre-Darwinian mythology and post-Darwinian nonsense." The virgin birth and Christ's divinity are "as traditionally understood, impossible." The New Testament miracles, he writes, "can no longer be interpreted in a post-Newtonian world as supernatural events performed by an incarnate deity." And the biblical view of the crucifixion "as the sacrifice for the sins of the world is a barbarian idea based on primitive concepts of God and must be dismissed." The resurrection, he says, "cannot be a physical resuscitation occurring inside human history." He dismisses the authority and integrity of Scripture as a standard for ethical behavior; he denies the effectiveness of prayer; he rejects the reality of heaven or hell.

In short, there is nothing identifiably Christian that would survive in his "new Christianity." He has redefined Christianity out of existence and replaced it with a belief system that denies everything Jesus and the apostles established and taught. This is simply an attempt to hijack the substance and institutional structure of Christianity while dismantling all its beliefs, values, doctrines, and traditions.[1]

This is nothing new. Secularists and apostates have been commandeering and subverting Christian churches and Christian institutions for centuries. Look at the history of the great educational institutions in America:

• Harvard University—the oldest institution of higher learning in the United States—was founded in 1636 in Cambridge, Massachusetts, and named New College. It was renamed after its principal donor, clergyman John Harvard, who donated half his property and his entire library of books to the institution. Harvard was originally founded to train young minds in the principles of God's Word. The school's original motto: "For Christ and the Church."

• Yale University in Connecticut was founded as a place where "youth may be instructed in the Arts and Sciences who through the blessing of Almighty God may be fit for employment both in the Church and Civil State."

• Brown University in Rhode Island was founded "to train ministers and educate youth properly in the Christian faith."

• Dartmouth College in New Hampshire was founded in 1769 with funds raised by a Native American preacher, Samson Occom, who wanted to educate young Native Americans in the Christian faith. The school's motto is *"Vox Clamantis in Deserto"* ("The voice of one crying in the wilderness"), the prophetic cry of John the Baptist.

• Boston University has kept the founders' motto of "Learning, Virtue, and Piety," even though virtue and piety disappeared long ago from the school's list of educational priorities.

• Amherst College in Massachusetts was founded as an institution for training young men to serve God. Its motto, *"Terras Irradient,"* refers to Isaiah 6:3: "The whole earth is full of His glory."

• Located in Massachusetts, Wellesley College was founded in 1875 as a women's college that would be "distinctly and positively Christian in its influence, discipline and instruction." Though Wellesley has kept its original motto, *"Non Ministrari sed Ministrare"* ("Not to be ministered unto but to minister"), the school is overwhelmingly anti-Christian in its teaching today.

 • Princeton University was founded in New Jersey in 1746 as a direct result of the revival of faith that followed the Great Awakening. The school's first president, Rev. Jonathan Dickinson, once said, "Cursed be all learning that is contrary to the cross of Christ."

The list goes on and on—one institution of higher learning after another, founded by Christians on Christian principles for Christian purposes. Every one of these institutions has been gradually taken over and subverted by secularists and apostates—false teachers with high-sounding words and treacherous intentions. What these schools have become, what they now teach, and what they permit to take place on their campuses, would shock and grieve the hearts of their founders.

In a similar way, Paul evangelized the Corinthian believers and founded the church in Corinth—then false teachers came in, seeking to subvert and take over the church. Presenting themselves as wiser and more godly than Paul, they proceeded to tear down Paul's reputation while teaching a false and destructive "gospel" among the people. The false teachers said, "We know the truth. We are progressive. We are moving with the times. Paul can't be trusted. His gospel is false. He's a wimp, he's wishy-washy."

Paul was the builder of the Corinthian church; he made the converts and invested the time to establish the Corinthians as disciples. The false teachers built nothing and established nothing. They moved in, hijacked the church Paul built, and proceeded to tear down both Paul and the Corinthian church.

Paul's answer to these false teachers and to anyone who followed them is: "Such people should realize that what we are in our letters when we are absent, we will be in our actions when we are present" (2 Cor. 10:11). In other words, "Look at the consistency of my life. Look at my commitment to Christ. Look at my lifestyle. I'm the same person in private and in public. I'm the same person in my letters as when I'm present. I am a man of integrity. I don't tear down. I build up."

Godly pride that boasts only in the Lord is a pride that shows mercy to people and a pride that builds up.

3. "Good Pride" Is Tenacious

Next, Paul tells us that "good pride" is persistent and tenacious. It does not give up. A person who boasts only in the Lord is not wishy-washy, nor is he a spineless wimp. He's tough in the face of opposition and criticism. He doesn't let go and give up when the wind is in his face, when he gets tired, when others around him want to quit. He boasts in the Lord, and He knows that the power of the Lord will give him a second wind—and if necessary, a third and a fourth wind. You can't defeat a Christian who boasts in the Lord. Knock him down a thousand times, and he'll get up 1001. He is determined to keep moving forward.

Yes, we are called to be meek and humble—but that doesn't mean we are to become doormats. We meekly but tenaciously stand for the truth. We humbly but persistently proclaim Christ in the midst of opposition and persecution. Humility does not mean surrender to the enemies of Christ. Meekness doesn't mean we fold up our tents and let the false teachers take over our platform, our microphone, our megaphone. No, we will assertively, tenaciously, and boldly brag about our Lord. Our reputation is nothing, but His is everything.

That is good, godly, humble pride. Our humility makes us boastful. We will brag day and night about who Jesus is. We will boast of the truth. We will proudly confess that His strength is perfected in our weakness, His power is manifested in our powerlessness. We utterly depend on Him and we surrender to Him.

I will never brag about my credentials—but I will *never stop* bragging about my Lord. As the Psalmist David said, "Some boast in chariots and some in horses, but we will boast in the name of the LORD, our God" (Ps. 20:7 NASB); and, "My soul will boast in the LORD; let the afflicted hear and rejoice" (Ps. 34:2).

Paul says, in effect, "I have pride in the Lord Who loved me, the Lord Who redeemed me, the Lord Who died and rose from the grave for me, the Lord Who gives me strength, power, and victory. He is my stronghold and my fortress."

Your Fortress

Scotland's most famous landmark is Edinburgh Castle, an ancient fortress on a volcanic crag overlooking the city of Edinburgh. There have been fortified strongholds on that rocky crag since the seventh century, but the present castle was built in the 1400s. The fortress is a visible symbol of impregnable strength—and there is only one time in its long history that Edinburgh Castle was ever captured by enemy forces.

Sir William Kirkcaldy commanded Edinburgh Castle during a yearlong siege from 1572 to 1573, when English forces of Queen Elizabeth I attempted to capture the fortress. The pride of Edinburgh Castle was a massive tower, called David's Tower, which had been built almost two centuries earlier by David II of Scotland, son of Scottish hero Robert the Bruce. David's Tower stood one hundred feet tall and housed the main entrance to the castle. Sir William and his fellow Scots considered the tower to be indestructible.

The English forces positioned cannons on a hill below the crag and took aim at the base of David's Tower—the symbol of Scottish pride and defiance. The bombardment began in May 1573 and lasted for ten days. The English cannonballs chipped away at the base of the tower until the entire massive stone structure collapsed under its own weight. The collapse blocked the castle's only source of water.

The very feature that made the stone tower seem so strong—its massive height and weight—proved to be its greatest weakness. Edinburgh Castle surrendered, Sir William was hanged, and the castle has remained under the authority of the English crown ever since.[2]

In our human foolishness, we all too often take pride in the very towers of human strength, human intellect, and human argument that are our greatest sources of weaknesses. In our pride, we place our trust in the weapons and fortifications of this world instead of God's omnipotent power.

Paul reminds us, "The weapons we fight with are not the weapons of the world. On the contrary, they have divine power to demolish strongholds. . . . But, 'Let him who boasts boast in the Lord.' For it is not the one who commends himself who is approved, but the one whom the Lord commends" (2 Cor. 10:4,17–18).

The Lord is our fortress. Proudly boast in Him . . . and experience the power of positive living.

When Jealousy Is a Virtue

Sir John Gielgud was one of the most acclaimed Shakespearean actors of the twentieth century. He was second only to Sir Laurence Olivier in fame and honors. On one occasion, Sir John was sitting with friends, discussing Shakespeare's *Othello*. In the tragic play, Othello's enemy, Iago, makes it appear Othello's new bride, Desdemona, has been unfaithful to him. In his jealousy, Othello murders Desdemona—then learns she was innocent.

Reflecting on Othello's murderous and mistaken jealousy, Sir John said, "It was hard for me to identify with Othello. I really don't know what jealousy feels like." He paused, as if he had experienced a moment of revelation, then he said, "I take that back! I have felt jealousy—once. When Larry Olivier had such a huge success in *Hamlet*, I wept!"

2 Corinthians 11:1–33

Ever since we were children, we've been taught jealousy is a sin. Yet we now come to the thirteenth secret of positive living: when jealousy is a virtue. Jealousy—a virtue? How can that be? How can jealousy, which has caused so much suffering in so many lives down through history, really be a virtue?

You are about to learn that there is such a thing as "godly jealousy" and this form of jealousy truly is a good thing. By practicing the virtue of godly jealousy, you will experience the power of positive living.

The place to begin is with God. From cover to cover, again and again, we read our God is a jealous God. One of His essential characteristics is His jealousy. In the second commandment, God says, "You shall not bow down to them or worship them; for I, the LORD your God, am a jealous God" (Exod. 20:5a). Joshua told the people that the Lord "is a holy God; he is a jealous God" (Josh. 24:19b). And in a passage discussing whether Christians should eat meat sacrificed to idols, Paul wrote, "Are we trying to arouse the Lord's jealousy?" (1 Cor. 10:22)

If godly jealousy belongs to the Lord, then you and I need to learn how to develop a godly jealousy. I can sense your skepticism as you read these words. And you *should* be skeptical. Don't ever accept any assertion made by any Christian author or preacher unless he can back it up with Scripture. The question is: what do the Scriptures say to us about godly jealousy?

Jealousy Versus Envy

One problem we have is with our understanding of the word "jealousy." We often use the words "jealousy" and "envy" interchangeably, but these two words do not mean the same thing. Envy is a desire to have something that belongs to another person. Jealousy is a desire not to lose something that belongs to you.

Envy is a sin. Authentic jealousy is not.

Let me illustrate: When a husband and wife are deeply in love with each other, they should zealously and jealously guard that special relationship, should they not? Exclusiveness is the very heart of marriage. Forsaking all others, these two should be as one. Jealousy means simply to guard what belongs exclusively to that relationship. In this sense, jealousy is not only right, it's a virtue. There would be something drastically wrong if these two people felt no jealous desire to keep themselves exclusively for each other.

Suppose a third person comes in and tries to intrude in their relationship—a former boyfriend or girlfriend, or some outsider who wants to seduce one partner or the other. What happens? Jealousy kicks in—as well it should. In a healthy marriage relationship, both partners will say, "This person cannot cross the boundary line we have drawn around our relationship. We will not allow any intruders into our marriage." If someone tried to transgress the boundary lines of the marriage, it would be wrong *not* to be jealous. The purpose of jealousy in a marriage relationship is to guard what belongs exclusively to a couple: emotional intimacy, sexual intimacy, love, and oneness.

Why do we have alarm systems in our homes, our cars, and our offices? We, as good stewards, seek to protect what is ours. We don't want someone to come in and steal what rightfully belongs to us. That is healthy jealousy in action. It would be negligent not to be jealous with regard to our family's goods and assets.

When Dean Rusk, the former secretary of state, was studying at Oxford University in England, he bought a little boat. He would take that boat out on the river to relax. At the end of the day, he'd pull the boat up out of the water and leave it on the shore.

One day, the boat was stolen. Within a week, authorities recovered the boat—and they arrested the thief who took it.

When they went to court, the judge ordered Rusk to pay a fine of ten pounds.

Rusk was stunned. "Your Honor!" he said. "I didn't steal the boat! The thief stole the boat from me!"

The judge replied, "I have fined you because, by leaving your boat unlocked, you were tempting a thief." Dean Rusk had to pay a fine because he did not behave jealously toward his boat.[1]

God's Love Protecting Itself

Our heavenly Father is jealous toward His children because His children are easily tempted into running off and going astray. Sometimes His children chase after idols and false gods. Sometimes they chase after false teachers and false religious ideas, or empty rituals or material possessions, or self-worship or the desire to "fit in" with the wrong crowd.

God feels jealousy whenever one of His children is led astray. Why? Because God is totally committed to you, His child. Total commitment involves a deep emotional investment. When you are unfaithful to God, when your love for Him grows cold, He becomes deeply hurt—and He becomes jealous. Why? Because you are His very own child, and His love for you is an exclusive love. He refuses to share your love with some false god or earthly thing.

You may be thinking, *Certainly, not all jealousy is good. Not all jealousy is godly. I know someone whose jealousy is driving him to insanity. He's insanely jealous. He imagines his wife is unfaithful, but she's not. He hires private detectives to have her followed. He has her phone tapped. He starts arguments and falsely accuses her. Certainly, you're not saying an insane jealousy is a virtue!*

No, I'm not saying that at all. The fact is, we human beings are fallen and subject to sin and error. Our judgment is distorted. We sometimes become insecure and suspicious. Because of sin and the flesh, our jealousy can become selfish, possessive, irrational, and suspicious. At that point, the virtue of healthy jealousy can turn into a sin and a sickness.

But not so with God's jealousy. The holy jealousy of God is pure, righteous, selfless, and perfect. He becomes jealous toward us because He loves us and wants the best for us.

Sometimes we say, "I wish God weren't so jealous! I wish He'd leave me alone to do what I want!" In our sinfulness and selfishness, we reject God's perfect, loving jealousy toward us. But if you love someone, you want the best for that person. God is not selfishly *possessive*; He's selflessly *protective*.

Why does God feel jealousy when we forsake Him? Because He is the all-knowing God. He knows when you are led away into the wilderness of unbelief or run after false teaching, the consequences in your life can be painful and even deadly. He loves you too much to let you bring lasting harm upon yourself. He knows when you fall into error, you will lose His power and blessing in your life. You will lose His hand of protection over your life.

That's why godly jealousy is not only a virtue but a power for positive living. As someone once said, "Jealousy is God's love protecting itself."

The Bridegroom and the Marriage Supper

In 2 Corinthians 11, we find that Paul exhibits a godly jealousy toward the Corinthian believers. They are Paul's children in the faith, and he loves them deeply. He feels a holy jealousy toward them when they stray from the faith and turn their backs on his teachings. The Corinthian Christians have been misled by false teachers, and Paul lovingly, and jealously wants to call them back to their first love, a true devotion to the Lord Jesus Christ.

He uses a beautiful word-picture of a Jewish marriage to make his point. He writes: "I hope you will put up with a little of my foolishness; but you are already doing that. I am jealous for you with a godly jealousy. I promised you to one husband, to Christ, so that I might present you as a pure virgin to him. But I am afraid that just as Eve was deceived by the serpent's cunning, your minds may somehow be led astray from your sincere and pure devotion to Christ" (2 Cor. 11:1-3).

In biblical times, an engagement was as legally binding as a marriage. An engaged couple were bound to each other by legal and social obligations so strong the only act left to the actual wedding night was the physical consummation of the union. Legally, the engaged couple were considered to be bound together as husband and wife from the moment they became engaged. The betrothal could only be broken by death or divorce.

During the time of betrothal, the bride waits anxiously and expectantly for the day of celebration. Throughout that period of waiting, the father is responsible to protect his daughter so he can present her to her betrothed bridegroom as a pure and virginal bride.

Paul is saying that, having led the Corinthians to the Lord and having founded the Corinthian church, he feels like he is the "father of the bride." He takes personal responsibility for their spiritual purity and faithfulness. He is their spiritual guardian and he is committed to presenting the Corinthian Christians as a pure and virginal bride to their Bridegroom, the Lord Jesus Christ. He is protecting the Corinthian believers until that great day of celebration when all believers meet the Bridegroom in glory.

That's why Paul jealously protects the Corinthians from false teachers and deceivers who seek to seduce them away from their first love, Jesus Christ. Many of us as believers fail to understand that when we come to Jesus and receive Him as Lord and Savior, we make a binding betrothal or engagement agreement with the Bridegroom. One day, after we have remained faithful and true to Him in this life, we'll celebrate the Marriage Supper of the Lamb, as described in the book of Revelation:

> Then I heard what sounded like a great multitude, like the roar of rushing waters and like loud peals of thunder, shouting:
>
> "Hallelujah!
> For our Lord God Almighty reigns.
> Let us rejoice and be glad
>   and give him glory!
> For the wedding of the Lamb has come,
>   and his bride has made herself ready.
> Fine linen, bright and clean,
>   was given her to wear."
> (Fine linen stands for the righteous acts of the saints.)
>
> Then the angel said to me, "Write: 'Blessed are those who are invited to the wedding supper of the Lamb!'" And he added, "These are the true words of God."
>
> *(Revelation 19:6-9)*

What a great celebration that will be! It will be the wedding of all weddings when the Bridegroom takes us by the hand and leads us into eternal glory.

Now you understand why Paul felt so heartsick when the believers he led into the Kingdom, his own spiritual children, were drifting away from the truth and being seduced by deceivers. This heartsickness was a sign of Paul's holy jealousy for the Corinthians.

Jealously Involved in Each Other's Lives

My wife and I have four children, two sons and two daughters. I have had the joy of walking both my daughters down the aisle of our church and presenting them to their bridegrooms, their husbands-to-be. Many thoughts went through my mind as I contemplated what it meant to give my daughters in marriage.

I remembered how my wife and I nurtured them as babies and how we stayed up with them through teething, colic, coughs, and fevers. I remembered how we taught them to walk and talk. I recalled the birthday parties and Christmas celebrations. I remembered teaching them how to ride their bikes, and helping them with their homework, and attending parent-teacher conferences. I recalled the hours spent driving them to various activities—and the small fortune we spent on orthodontists and college tuition. And I recalled how I felt as a helpless passenger when my daughters were each learning to drive.

I thought: *I went through all that—just for the joy of handing my daughters over to their husbands? Was it worth it?*

And the answer: Yes! It was worth every bit of it. Those two times I placed my daughters' hands in the hands of their handsome young men, I was overjoyed because of the fact our family was growing. I wasn't losing two daughters, I was gaining two sons. And the joy I felt was indescribable!

In 2 Corinthians 11, Paul talks about a similar joy. He has gone through many sufferings. He has made many sacrifices. He has worried, agonized, and toiled so he might one day present the Corinthian church as a spotless and virginal bride to the Bridegroom in heaven.

As we read through the two letters Paul wrote to the Corinthians, we see he sometimes had to rebuke the Corinthians, as a father must sometimes rebuke a straying child. He admonished them out of love, because he wanted to preserve their purity and faithfulness. He was jealous to present the Corinthians to the Bridegroom as a spotless and undefiled bride. His jealousy is an example to you and me.

My friend, it is not wrong to feel jealousy when we see a fellow believer straying from the faith into unbelief or error. That is a holy and loving jealousy. There may be a few spiritually immature people who, upon seeing you jealously restoring an erring brother or sister, would call you "judgmental." But just tell them, "I love my brothers and sisters with a godly jealousy. The love of Christ won't let me stand idle while my fellow Christian falls away. It would be so much easier to be apathetic and uninvolved—but I choose to concern myself with the things that concern God. I'm not judgmental. I'm jealous, and my jealousy is a godly jealousy."

Now you can see why expressing jealousy for the truth and for the saints is one of the fifteen secrets for positive living. Godly jealousy requires us to watch out for one another, to serve one another, to love one another enough to confront one another. It means we refuse to live in selfish isolation from each other. Instead, we choose to be lovingly, jealously involved in each other's lives. As Paul said:

> But I am afraid that just as Eve was deceived by the serpent's cunning, your minds may somehow be led astray from your sincere and pure devotion to Christ. For if someone comes to you and preaches a Jesus other than the Jesus we preached, or if you receive a different spirit from the one you received, or a different gospel from the one you accepted, you put up with it easily enough. . . . For such men are false apostles, deceitful workmen, masquerading as apostles of Christ. And no wonder, for Satan himself masquerades as an angel of light. It is not surprising, then, if his servants masquerade as servants of righteousness. Their end will be what their actions deserve.

(2 Corinthians 11:3–4, 13–15)

Where do false teachers come from? Satan himself sends them into the church. Just as Satan masquerades as an angel of light, these false apostles masquerade as apostles of Christ. They pretend to be the real deal. They may have the title "Reverend" in front of their names and a string of degrees behind. They may stand in the pulpits dressed in clerical garb, waving a Bible about as they speak. But if they do not proclaim that Jesus was God in human flesh, the crucified sacrifice for our sin, buried and risen again, the only way to the Father and to heaven—they are false teachers and false apostles.

It's time for us to be vigilant. It's time for us to understand the virtue of jealousy. As our world grows darker and more dangerous, more and more believers are being seduced and lured away from faithfulness to Christ. We must put an end to compromise and apathy. We must begin to use this holy jealousy, this thirteenth secret of positive living, as a tool with which to bless one another and encourage one another to press on, and press on, and press on into the Kingdom.

Be holy and be jealous for Christ and His body, the church. Be faithfully jealous and jealously faithful, and you will see an exciting revival in your life and in your church beyond anything you dare to imagine.

SECRET NUMBER 14

Stars Instead of Scars

Joseph Addison was an English political leader and writer, the author of the play *Cato, a Tragedy*. He was also a devout Christian and a champion of human liberty. For many years, Addison was deeply concerned about his carousing, rebellious stepson. On many occasions, Addison urged his stepson to repent of his lifestyle and turn his life over to God—all to no avail.

According to historian Samuel Johnson, when Joseph Addison knew he was dying, he called the young man to his deathbed for one final appeal. "I have sent for you," Addison said, "that you may see in what peace a Christian can die." Those were Joseph Addison's last words.

Johnson concludes that no one knows what effect Addison's words had on the stepson, because "he likewise died himself in a short time."[1]

2 Corinthians
11:16—12:10

No matter how young or how old we are, we all face trials and tragedies in life. In our youth, we face the bully in the school yard. As we grow older, we face sorrows, losses, conflict, failure, opposition, depression, loneliness, illness—and sooner or later, we face the last enemy, death itself. Then we discover the truth of Joseph Addison's last words: "See in what peace a Christian can die."

A Thorn in the Flesh

We all suffer the blows and pain of life. Sometimes we mistakenly refer to our difficulties and trials as a "thorn in the flesh." I say "mistakenly" because, when Paul in 2 Corinthians 12 spoke of "a thorn in the flesh," he was not talking about the normal array of difficulties and trials that are a part of every human life. The things we are so quick to call a "thorn in the flesh" usually do not fit the biblical defnition.

How do I know this? I know it because Paul faced more physical suffering and mental anguish than most people face in ten lifetimes—yet he never referred to any of the sufferings he endured as a "thorn in the flesh." In this passage, Paul speaks of having been imprisoned, flogged, and repeatedly exposed to death; then he gives us this list of his sufferings:

> Five times I received from the Jews the forty lashes minus one. Three times I was beaten with rods, once I was stoned, three times I was shipwrecked, I spent a night and a day in the open sea, I have been constantly on the move. I have been in danger from rivers, in danger from bandits, in danger from my own countrymen, in danger from Gentiles; in danger in the city, in danger in the country, in danger at sea; and in danger from false brothers. I have labored and toiled and have often gone without sleep; I have known hunger and thirst and have often gone without food; I have been cold and naked. Besides

everything else, I face daily the pressure of my concern for all the churches. Who is weak, and I do not feel weak? Who is led into sin, and I do not inwardly burn?

(2 Corinthians 11:24-29)

That is an astounding catalog of pain and scars, all suffered by this one human being, the apostle Paul—yet he never called any of those painful experiences a "thorn in the flesh." Why? Because this term, a "thorn in the flesh," has a specific meaning, and when Paul speaks of this "thorn," he associates it with great blessing from the Lord.

Paul was greatly privileged and honored by God. He had the privilege of meeting the resurrected Lord in person through his conversion experience on the Damascus road. Later, in 2 Corinthians 12:1, Paul speaks of having received "visions and revelations from the Lord." He had the privilege of being taken up into heaven, where he was shown things he could not even describe in human language. He was shown all the glories of heaven and became a living witness to spiritual realities that perhaps no other human being, besides Isaiah and John, had ever seen in his mortal lifetime. Paul said that all of this honor and privilege went to his head.

But the Lord made it possible for Paul to experience these privileges while keeping his humility. The Lord permitted Paul to be afflicted by a "thorn in the flesh" for a very specific purpose. Paul wrote, "To keep me from becoming conceited because of these surpassingly great revelations, there was given me a thorn in my flesh, a messenger of Satan, to torment me" (2 Corinthians 12:7).

The word "thorn" here is the Greek word *"skolops,"* meaning *splinter* or *barb*, like the barb on the end of a fishing hook. It suggests something sharp and painful when it penetrates. The Greek word translated as "flesh" is *"sarx,"* which does not necessarily refer to the physical body. The word *"sarx"* appears more than 150 times in the New Testament, and often refers to the physical body, but is used more often to refer to our fallen "fleshly" nature resulting from Adam's sin. In 2 Corinthians 12, however, Paul uses the word *"sarx"* to refer specifically to his own inner being. This "thorn" caused Paul suffering in his inner man, and this suffering kept him humble so God could use him in a mighty way.

What, specifically, was Paul's "thorn"? Was it a physical ailment or abnormality? Bible scholars have debated this question for centuries and have speculated that Paul was afflicted with one of these physical conditions: migraines, chronic eye problems, speech impediment, malaria, epilepsy, gallstones, gout, rheumatism, intestinal disorder, and on and on. But there is nothing in the text to indicate that Paul's "thorn" was necessarily physical in nature. Given all the physical punishment and suffering he endured over the years, I tend to discount the theory that his "thorn" was physical in nature.

When you read Paul's letters, you can hear a great deal of anguish in his words—but it's not physical anguish. The greatest pain Paul suffered was caused by the defection and betrayal of his friends. A beating is just a beating—but when the Corinthian Christians believed lies about him and rejected him, he was devastated. He had trouble letting go of the pain inflicted on him by fellow believers, by his children in the faith. When the people you trust, the people you count on, suddenly turn on you for no reason or for false reasons, that is torture to your soul. It can cause you much more intense suffering than mere physical pain.

We don't know whether Paul's "thorn" was physical or emotional. We only know it was extremely painful and probably humiliating, since it was given to him by God in order to keep him humble. It was probably something buried so deep no one else could see it or understand it, not even those closest to Paul.

But the apostle Paul felt it constantly. It was with him wherever he went. It throbbed and nagged at him, continually reminding him not to become conceited. It was something so terrible he couldn't talk about it to anyone except the Lord.

I'm sure there's a good reason the Scriptures do not tell us the exact nature of Paul's "thorn in the flesh." The Holy Spirit deliberately kept this information from us so we would be able to identify with Paul even if our "thorn" came in a different package than Paul's. Whether you are going through physical pain, emotional pain, relational pain, personal problems, financial problems, or opposition from difficult people, you can observe how Paul dealt with his "thorn" and you can learn from him. The problem is not the pain, but how you respond to the pain; it's not the trials of life that matter, but how you handle those trials.

What Is Your *"Thorn"?*

The important thing is not what our "thorn" *is* but how we *respond* to it. How do you deal with your "thorn in the flesh"? What is your attitude toward it? How do you live every day with a humbling, throbbing "thorn" in your flesh that keeps you from becoming conceited and self-important? Most important of all, how do you use your "thorn" as a stepping-stone to blessings?

It makes no difference what your "thorn" is, but it makes all the difference in the world how you respond to it. Do you choose to live negatively or positively? One thing is certain: when you face a situation that will not change, even after pleading with God in prayer, then you are going to have to allow that situation to change *you*.

The fourteenth secret of positive living is: seeing stars instead of scars. Understanding this secret can mean the difference between a life of joy—or a life of sadness. It can mean the difference between living a life empowered and effective—or a life of frustration and regret. It can mean the difference between victorious living—and a life of defeat.

You are God's child, and His love for you is unchangeable. His commitment to you is permanent. He never gives up on you. Since God has such an intense commitment to His children, what must He do to get the attention of a child whose ego is out of control? What must He do to get the attention of a child who has begun to take His grace for granted, who takes credit for what God has graciously provided, who takes and takes yet gives nothing back but crumbs?

God tries and tries to reach His erring child, but the child is not listening. Finally, God does the only thing He can do: He permits Satan to bring a "thorn" into that child's life. What kind of "thorn" will it be? Whatever it takes to get that child's attention.

And please understand this: What God would need to do to get my attention might be altogether different from what He must do to get your attention. We are all different. The "thorn" that God might allow in my life might not be at all like the "thorn" in your life. But one way or another, He *will* get your attention. Once you are attentive to Him and the things He wishes to teach you, two things will happen:

1. You will experience humility.
2. God will be glorified.

Now, God doesn't want you to live in fear that some awful "thorn" is about to invade your life. He does not take pleasure in our pain. He will only allow a "thorn" in our lives when all else has failed.

As we look at this issue of a "thorn in the flesh" and apply Paul's teaching to our own lives, we have to ask ourselves several questions:

- Do I have a "thorn in the flesh" right now?
- Am I qualified to get a "thorn" in the future?
- Do I meet the conditions for a "thorn"?
- What do I have to do to get a "thorn"—or more to the point, what must I do to *avoid* getting one?

If you conclude you don't have a thorn in your flesh right now, let me encourage you to *never* pray for one. There must be two factors at work in your life for you to get a "thorn in the flesh." The first factor: God has to have blessed you abundantly and overwhelmingly, as He blessed the apostle Paul. The second factor: you must have allowed these blessings to go to your head and make you prideful.

What Paul Teaches About "Thorns"

The key questions are: How did Paul handle his pain? What can we learn from his example? Did he feel thrilled and blessed that God gave him this "thorn in the flesh"?

You may say, "Michael, don't be ridiculous. Paul clearly wasn't happy about his 'thorn.' No sane person would be happy about chronic suffering." That's true. But I have actually heard Christians offer glib counsel to people who are going through intense pain, loss, or suffering: "Oh, you should be happy that you're going through this. Isn't it wonderful God has found you worthy to go through this experience. You should be grateful to have cancer, or to have gone bankrupt, or to have this paralyzing accident."

What foolishness! Look again at the example of Paul. He didn't go around saying, "Praise the Lord! I have a thorn in the flesh!" No! He cried out to God, begging Him to remove it. Paul writes, "Three times I pleaded with the Lord to take it away from me" (2 Cor. 12:8). That doesn't mean Paul prayed about the matter three times, then said, "Oh, well." I'm sure each of those times was an extended and intense period of wrestling with God in prayer. He desperately wanted to be free of this chronic and crippling "thorn" in his life. Each of those prayer sessions probably involved days of fasting and meditating and imploring God with tears and intense emotion.

Finally, after the third time, Paul received his answer from the Lord. Paul described God's reply in these words: "But [God] said to me, 'My grace is sufficient for you, for my power is made perfect in weakness'" (2 Cor. 12:9a).

Once Paul received his answer from the Lord, how did he respond? Somehow he was able to move from an attitude of "God, free me from this pain!" to an attitude of "God, I delight in weakness and hardship for Your sake!" But how did he get there? How did Paul turn his scars into stepping-stones to blessing?

It began when Paul heard God say to him, "My grace is sufficient for you, for my power is made perfect in weakness." The Lord ministered to Paul in his pain and weakness, revealing a truth to Paul we all need to understand. It is normal and human to pray as Paul prayed, "God, please get me out of this. Take this away from me. Rescue me!" After all, Jesus prayed the same prayer to the Father the night before He was crucified, "Father, if you are willing, take this cup from me" (see Luke 22:42).

Of course, we tend to leave off the rest of Jesus' prayer: "yet not my will, but yours be done." When we pray, "Lord, get me out of this," we don't want to hear any answer from God except, "Yes, sir," or "Yes, ma'am."

The example of Jesus and the example of Paul prove that there's nothing wrong with asking God to remove us and rescue us from a bad situation. But we have to be open to the Lord's answer—even if the answer is "No." When Paul prayed that prayer, the Lord answered, "My grace is sufficient for you—even for this 'thorn' that won't go away. My power is perfectly demonstrated not in human strength, but in human weakness."

I don't know how Paul heard that answer. He may have actually heard God's voice speaking to him. Perhaps the answer came to him in a vision or a dream. Or perhaps, when Paul saw his circumstances weren't changing even after three intense prayer sessions, he interpreted God's answer from his situation and his circumstances. Paul doesn't explain in what exact form God's answer came to him—but Paul had no doubt the answer was from God.

When Paul realized God had answered "no" to his prayer for the "thorn" to be removed, he came to a conclusion. In effect, Paul decided, "God must want me to brag about my weaknesses, not my strengths." We human beings are always ready to brag about our strengths and successes, but the chronic "thorn" that afflicted Paul convinced him he should brag about his weakness instead.

Put another way, Paul concluded: "I'm not going to dwell upon my scars. I am not going to have a pity party for my scars. I am not going to weep and moan, 'Oh, woe is me.' I'm not going to mope and feel sorry for myself. I'm going to view my scars as God views them. God is not bashing me, He's not blasting me, He's blessing me with this 'thorn.' It hurts—but it's making me a stronger, more Christlike, more humble person. If I didn't have this 'thorn,' I'd be tempted to brag about my strengths and accomplishments. But because of this 'thorn,' I'm going to brag about God's strengths and all the things He is accomplishing through my weakness."

That is what God continually seeks to do in our lives: He is trading our scars for stars. He is teaching us to take our eyes off our wounds so we can look up in wonder and see the cosmic grandeur of His plan for our lives. Our "thorns" are truly the doorway to God's supernatural power in our lives—if we will learn how to look at them.

Has your "thorn" created a deep disappointment in your life? Then it's time for you to allow God to transform that disappointment into a divine appointment for His power to be displayed in your life. Has your "thorn" left a feeling of unfulfillment in your life? Then allow God to fulfill His promises to you. Is your "thorn" a trial of suffering and anguish? Then offer it to God and allow Him to manifest His healing in your life. Does your "thorn" make you feel like a failure? Then let God's power and success be manifested through your weakness and failure.

In the summer of 1907, a young Norwegian-born American named Ole was in a rowboat with his girlfriend, Bess, on a Wisconsin lake. They rowed out to an island to have a picnic together. It was a warm day, and they sat in the shade of a tree, talking and sharing lunch together. Finally, Bess said, "Ole, do you know what would make this moment perfect?"

"What's that?"

"Ice-cream sundaes."

Ice-cream sundaes! It would mean having to row the boat to the town on the shore, buying ice cream at the drugstore, then rowing back to the island—at least a twenty-minute round-trip. But Ole was in love and he was glad to do anything for Bess. So, leaving Bess at their shady spot on the island, he rowed back to the shore, bought a pint of vanilla ice cream, and rowed back.

When he reached the island, Bess looked at the ice-cream carton and said, "Where's the chocolate syrup? It wouldn't be sundaes without chocolate syrup."

So Ole got back into the boat and rowed toward shore for chocolate syrup. This time, however, he was not as happy to make the trip as he was the first time. All this rowing was making him hot and tired. He silently grumbled, *If Bess had wanted chocolate syrup, she should have asked for chocolate syrup!*

Suddenly, an idea came to Ole. He stopped rowing, pulled the oars out of the water—and he thought. And he thought. He was so absorbed in his thinking that more than an hour passed and Ole wasn't even aware of the passage of time.

Finally, he remembered the time—and he realized he was in trouble with his girlfriend. He rowed back to the island, where he found Bess fuming and ready to break up with him. He quickly explained that the ice-cream errands had given him an idea that would make millions!

Ole went to work, and the following year, he began selling his invention—the first outboard motor for small boats. Bess not only forgave him, but she eventually married Ole Evinrude, the founder of the company that became Outboard Marine Corporation, manufacturer of Evinrude Outboard Motors. Ole Evinrude turned a "thorny" chore of rowing across the lake for ice cream into a multimillion-dollar business enterprise.[2]

You, too, can turn scars into stars. Whatever your scars may be, let God lift your eyes to the stars. Yours is a heavenly destiny. Ask Him to reveal His power and promises to you. Offer Him your "thorns" and watch Him reveal His glory—thus experiencing the power of positive living.

SECRET NUMBER 15

Ready for the Exam

Remember when you were in school? There was always one teacher who had a habit of walking into the classroom and announcing a surprise test. Oh, that teacher claimed surprise tests would ferret out those students who were always prepared versus those who were not.

2 Corinthians 13:1–14

But I never liked that kind of teacher—and with good reason. I was the kind of student who always crammed at the last minute. I would cram a whole year's worth of knowledge into two weeks of study. I didn't do well on surprise tests because if I didn't have two weeks' warning, I didn't have a chance to cram.

Now, the apostle Paul is a great teacher—and I must tell you, he's my kind of teacher. He doesn't delight in giving surprise exams. No, he's the kind of teacher who goes over the curriculum again and again. He patiently

prepares you for the test. He gives you hints about what questions will be on the exam. He waits until you reach the end of the epistle and you are thoroughly prepared, then he says, "Exam time!"

Ask any average student whether he or she likes exams. Most students will say they could easily live without them. But exams and tests are the only way to determine where a student stands and what that student has learned. They are the means of ascertaining success or failure, knowledge or ignorance, competence or incompetence.

That is why so many professions—whether law, medicine, or accounting—require board exams and board certifications. And thank God for that. Can you imagine if anyone could become a brain surgeon without having to pass a rigorous exam? What a disaster that would be.

In the spiritual life, there are also exams and tests. These examinations are self-administered. You don't get a letter grade— yet these tests entail greater consequences than anything else you will do in your life. The results of these exams and tests can determine your eternal destiny—an eternity in heaven or an eternity in hell.

The results of this exam reveal whether or not you will hear the Lord Jesus say to you, "Come, you who are blessed by the Father; take your inheritance, the kingdom prepared for you since the creation of the world"—or those terrifying words, "Depart from Me, you who are cursed, into the eternal fire prepared for the devil and his angels."

I can tell you with all certainty the most dangerous place for an unbeliever to be is in the church. The most dangerous place for a person to be is where he or she can hear the truth on a regular basis, yet continue to live apart from that truth. Those who hear the truth—but ignore it and reject it—bring greater judgment upon themselves. God will hold them accountable for the truth they have heard and rejected.

That is why we owe it to ourselves to examine ourselves, to test ourselves, to see if we are truly in the faith—or if we are in terrible spiritual danger. I hope you are ready, my friend. It's exam time.

Lowering the Standards

Here we come to the fifteenth and final secret of positive living. This is the final exam. Paul writes, "Examine yourselves to see whether you are in the faith; test yourselves. Do you not realize that Christ Jesus is in you—unless, of course, you fail the test? And I trust that you will discover that we have not failed the test" (2 Cor. 13:5–6).

The Corinthian Christians fell into the same trap that catches many educators today. They began to say, "If the students are not passing their exams, then change the curriculum. The course must be too difficult. The standards must be too high. We should stop insisting on accountability from our students. If we just lower the standards, the students will be able to pass their exams."

Many churches today are taking this same attitude: "The standards Jesus set are too high. People don't want to believe Jesus is the only way to heaven. Let them choose to believe what they want. After all, Jesus sounds intolerant and narrow-minded when He says, 'No one comes to the Father but by Me.' We don't want to offend anybody. We need to lower the standards, water down the truth, stop focusing on sin and repentance and salvation, and start focusing on self-esteem and inclusiveness and thinking positive thoughts."

Years ago, when I spent some time in Australia, I had to learn the rules for playing rugby and cricket. Not once did the officials of those games say to me, "Mr. Youssef, you're new to this country. You're a seeker of the game, so we'll simplify the rules for you. We'll lower the standards and change the rules for you." No, I had to play according to the official rules of the game.

Later, when I moved from Australia to America, I had to learn two entirely new games. They don't play rugby and cricket in America. They play American football and baseball. I didn't know the rules of those games, but at least I knew which direction the ball should go. It would have been much more tolerant and open-minded if the football and baseball leagues had said, "Mr. Youssef, you're new to the game, so we're going to make exceptions for you. We're going to lower the standards and change the rules for you." But that never happened.

You don't change the rules of rugby and cricket, football and baseball, just to be more open-minded and accommodating to new people. You can't have a game in which different people play by different rules because some are new to the game. The game is what it is and the rules are what they are, and each player must play by the same rules as every other player.

Why, then, do some people want to change the gospel, rewrite the Bible, edit the words of Jesus? Should we make people feel more comfortable in church at the expense of their eternal souls? Wouldn't it be better to tell them the uncomfortable truth now in order to spare them a hellish eternity later?

Some people want to replace the truth with happy thoughts and positive thinking: "Let's only have positive messages go out from our pulpits. Let's make sure people know they won't hear any nasty old sermons on sin and morality and eternal punishment here. Ours will be a church filled with only nice, happy, positive thoughts."

Compromising the truth may help people think happy, positive thoughts, but it can never produce positive living. If we accommodate our gospel to the culture of this dying world, our message will only lead people into error, delusion, false hopes, frustration, and, ultimately, hell itself. If we water down the message of Jesus and the reality of Jesus, we may help people to temporarily salve their consciences—but we will also succeed in destroying their souls.

Paul says if we want to experience truly positive living, true peace and joy, and a reliable assurance of heaven, then we must examine ourselves. We must test ourselves and make sure our salvation is genuine. We need to continually examine ourselves to see if we are still living according to the truth—or if we have moved away from the truth.

God will not change the rules to suit you. He will not grade on a curve. This test is strictly pass or fail. As King David wrote, "Search me, O God, and know my heart; test me and know my anxious thoughts. See if there is any offensive way in me, and lead me in the way everlasting" (Ps. 139:23-24).

Heads You Win, Tails You Win

Who should regularly examine themselves to see if they are in the faith? Was Paul warning a small group of apostates and false believers in the Corinthian church? No, Paul was urging *all of us as believers* to undertake a regular self-examination to see that we are walking faithfully with Christ. There are no exceptions. Every single person who claims to be a Christian should take this test.

Those who refuse or neglect to examine themselves are either dangerously arrogant or dangerously complacent. They are taking God and His salvation for granted—and they are placing their eternal souls at risk.

Moreover, we should want to examine ourselves, because there is good news for all who obediently put themselves to the test: When you take this exam, you can always be a winner. Everyone can succeed in this examination. Even those who fail can succeed. It's a case of, "Heads you win—tails you win!"

How can that be? How can you be a winner no matter how well—or how poorly—you do on the test? I'll explain.

If you examine yourself and find that you are in the faith, you will be overjoyed. You'll rejoice and give thanks to God. Heads—you win!

And if you examine yourself and find you are *not* in the faith, or you have moved *away* from the faith, you can repent, return to God, and come back to the faith—you won't be turned away. God has promised to receive you, accept you, forgive you, and restore you. Tails—you win!

The only losers in this test are those who know the truth, who discover they are not in the faith, and then refuse to change direction. But Paul did not expect the process of self-examination to produce losers. When he urged the Corinthians to examine themselves, he was confident they would win, that they would pass the test: "Examine yourselves to see whether you are in the faith; test yourselves. Do you not realize that Christ Jesus is in you—unless, of course, you fail the test?" (2 Cor. 13:5)

Jesus Christ dwells in the heart of every person who receives Him as their only Lord and Savior. That reality is our only hope for heaven. You may ask, "What is the proof Christ dwells in me? How do I know I have passed the test and I'm eternally saved? How can I be certain when I close my eyes in death, I will open them in heaven?"

The answer: a transformed life.

There is no more convincing evidence of salvation than the evidence of a transformed life. A young man who grew up on the shores of Lake Pontchartrain in southeastern Louisiana recalled how his life was changed when he saw Christ in the transformed life of his father, a fisherman:

My father was a Christian man. No matter how hard making a living fishing was, he never failed to give God credit for anything good, and he had ultimate faith that God was going to see us through when things were bad. I didn't pay much attention to his attempts to lead me to faith in Jesus when I was growing up. But after Papa died, I attended church and listened to the preacher describe Jesus and tell about His life. I was amazed and moved. I realized I'd already known a man like [Jesus]—my Papa.[1]

When people can see Jesus living in our transformed lives, they know our faith is real—and they are attracted by our life of authentic faith. When Jesus lives His life through our lives, we know we have been transformed—and we know we have passed the test.

Malcolm Muggeridge was an English socialist, atheist, journalist, and self-confessed womanizer. In 1968, he interviewed a Catholic nun about her work among the poor in Calcutta, India. He produced a book and a film about this nun, both of which were titled *Something Beautiful for God*. The book and film made the nun and her work world-famous. The nun's name was Mother Teresa. The evidence of her Christlike life convinced Muggeridge that Jesus was the way, the truth, and the life. At the age of sixty-five, he gave his life to Christ and was changed from a hardened atheist to a convinced believer.

From then on, everything about Malcolm Muggeridge was transformed: his lifestyle, his writings, and even his politics. In 1969, he published his first Christian book, *Jesus Rediscovered*; a few years later, he published a book called *Jesus: The Man Who Lives*. He wrote critically about his own past life as an atheist and a socialist, and he called his two-volume autobiography *Chronicles of Wasted Time* (1973). Reflecting on his conversion to Christ, Muggeridge said he felt "a sense of homecoming, of picking up the threads of a lost life, of responding to a bell that has long been ringing, of finding a place at a table that has long been left vacant."[2]

As we examine our own lives, we must look for evidence that Jesus Christ lives within us. We must look for evidence of a life transformed by the life of Christ within us. Christlikeness is the most reliable indicator of the reality of our salvation. If we examine ourselves and find no evidence of Christlikeness, then we have to question whether we are truly saved.

How to Take the Test

If you fail the test, if you are not living in the faith, then your life is meaningless. You'll live for a few years—then die and face the final judgment. It will be better for you in that day if you had never lived at all. Without a relationship with Jesus Christ, life has no purpose. No matter what you accomplish—how much wealth, fame, status, and achievement you accumulate—it ultimately comes to nothing if you have no personal relationship with Jesus Christ. That is what makes life worth living, period. So it is vitally important that we test ourselves and make certain we are in the faith.

You may ask, "How do I take this exam? How do I test myself to know whether I'm in the faith or not? Would my profession of faith many years ago prove I'm in the faith?"

Not necessarily.

You may say, "I prayed 'the sinner's prayer' many years ago. I confessed my sin and trusted Jesus as my Savior. Doesn't that mean I'm in the faith?"

Not necessarily.

You may say, "I've been baptized. I've joined the church. I attend church every Sunday. Doesn't that mean I'm in the faith?"

Not necessarily.

You may say, "I believe Jesus is the Son of God, that He is the way, the truth, and the life, and no one comes to the Father but by Him. Doesn't that prove I'm in the faith?"

Not necessarily.

As good as all of these things may be, they are not necessarily the authentic markers of being in the faith. Making a profession of faith is a good start. So is praying "the sinner's prayer." But Jesus Himself said, in the Parable of the Sower, that the "seed" of the gospel message will sometimes fall upon hearts like rocky ground. Jesus explained some people "receive the word with joy when they hear it, but they have no root. They believe for a while, but in the time of testing they fall away" (see Luke 8:13). So if you are relying on a past profession of faith, when you once received the word of the gospel with joy, you may be relying on a false hope.

What about baptism, church membership, and church attendance? These are all outward signs—but they should not be confused with the inward reality. There are many people who attend church religiously, who carry out all sorts of religious activities, who are baptized members in good standing of Bible-believing churches, but who do not belong to Jesus Christ. The Lord Jesus Himself said, "Not everyone who says to me, 'Lord, Lord,' will enter the kingdom of heaven, but only he who does the will of my Father who is in heaven" (see Matthew 7:21).

What about having sound biblical doctrines and believing all the right things about Jesus? The Scriptures tell us, "You believe that there is one God. Good! Even the demons believe that—and shudder" (James 2:19). Demons know sound doctrine. Their knowledge of Jesus Christ and the Bible surpasses the knowledge of any human being. But the demons aren't saved by their biblical knowledge, their doctrinal understanding. They are terrified of the judgment of God—a judgment they are doomed to suffer. A knowledge of doctrine and biblical truth is a good thing, but it does not save you.

The demons know what the Bible says about their future and they can't do anything about it. But you and I can choose whether we will live eternally or suffer eternal death. We can examine ourselves to see if we are in the faith—and if we find we come up short in any way, we can go to God in prayer and settle the matter right on the spot.

Four Key Questions

Let me suggest to you four key questions by which you may examine your own spiritual condition and test yourself to see if you are in the faith:

EXAM QUESTION 1:

"Am I eager to confess my sins and seek forgiveness?"

Do you confess your sins—or rationalize and explain your sins away? For example, when you know you have sinned, do you say things like, "I couldn't help it. I was under pressure." Or, "I'm only human. Anyone would have given in to temptation under the same circumstances." Or, "Everybody's doing it." The Psalmist expressed a godly attitude toward sin—an attitude of sorrow and mourning: "I confess my iniquity; I am troubled by my sin" (Ps. 38:18).

Those who mourn over their sin will be comforted. Those who confess their sins will obtain mercy and forgiveness. Confession of sin produces healing, peace, and joy. Some people claim confessing sin harms one's self-esteem—but in reality it is the *refusal* to confess our sin and receive God's cleansing forgiveness that harms the human mind, heart, and soul. The Psalmist spoke from his own experience when he wrote, "When I kept silent, my bones wasted away through my groaning all day long. For day and night your hand was heavy upon me; my strength was sapped as in the heat of summer" (Ps. 32:3-4).

But with confession, comes cleansing forgiveness, freedom from guilt, a restored relationship with God, and the positive assurance of salvation. The Psalmist continues, "Then I acknowledged my sin to you and did not cover up my iniquity.

I said, 'I will confess my transgressions to the LORD'—and you forgave the guilt of my sin" (Ps. 32:5).

If you avoid honestly facing and confessing your sin, then you should question whether you are truly in the faith. But if you eagerly seek God's cleansing forgiveness for your sins, you will experience the assurance of salvation.

EXAM QUESTION 2:

"Do I hunger and thirst for righteousness?"

Jesus said in the Sermon on the Mount, "Blessed are those who hunger and thirst for righteousness, for they will be filled" (Matt. 5:6). Hungering and thirsting for righteousness does not mean you are perfect or you will never fail. But it does mean you feel a disgust toward sin and a longing for righteousness. This is a reliable indicator of whether or not you are in the faith.

The Pharisees who opposed Jesus had many rules and rituals they made the people follow. They did all the right things outwardly, but they had no inward longing for righteousness. Outwardly, they practiced their religion to the letter; inwardly, they were filled with hatred and they plotted to murder Jesus because He threatened their power and their popularity.

If your faith is genuine, you will desire to obey God's Word whether people are watching you or not, whether people oppose you or applaud you, whether people appreciate you or castigate you. If you know that you hunger and thirst for righteousness, you can be assured you are truly in the faith.

EXAM QUESTION 3:

"Do I submit myself to the authority of God's Word?"

Do you willingly submit to God's authority—or do you try to explain away your rebellion or neglect of God's Word with such excuses as: "The Bible doesn't apply to life in these times," or, "I'm saved by grace. God will forgive me no matter what I do," or, "I don't want people to think of me as one of those religious fanatics."

If you are making excuses like these, then you are in a state of extreme spiritual danger. Jesus said, "If you love me, you will obey what I command" (John 14:15). He did not say, "Obey my commandments if it's not too much trouble," or, "Obey my commandments—unless people will think you're odd and not cool," or, "Obey my commandments, except when sin would be profitable and fun." No, He said, "Obey what I command," period.

If you disobey God's commandments and reject the authority of God's Word over your life, you do not love the Lord. If you do not love Him, how can you say you belong to Him? Jesus Himself stated clearly that obeying His Word is a sure sign you are in the faith: "If you hold to my teaching, you are really my disciples" (see John 8:31).

EXAM QUESTION 4:

"Do I genuinely love God and others?"

The apostle John put it this way: "This is how we know that we love the children of God: by loving God and carrying out his commands. This is love for God: to obey his commands. And his commands are not burdensome" (1 John 5:2-3).

The proof of our genuine faith is our love for the Lord. And John does not let us glibly say, "Oh yes, I love God! I think God is awesome!" He defines what love for God is—and he takes us right back to obedience: "This is love for God: to obey his commands." How do you express your love for God? Not just in words, but in acts of tangible, sacrificial, daily obedience.

The apostle John goes on to say if we are truly in the faith, then we will show it by our love for others, especially our brothers and sisters in Christ. He writes, "We know that we have passed from death to life, because we love our brothers. Anyone who does not love remains in death" (1 John 3:14).

That phrase "we have passed from death to life" is another way of saying we are in the faith, we are truly saved. Anyone who does not love others "remains in death," and is outside the faith. There's no use saying you're a believer, a follower of Christ, if your heart is full of hatred and bitterness. To be a follower of Christ means to live as He lived—and to love as He loved.

So examine yourself. Ask yourself these four questions. And remember, heads you win, tails you win. If your answer to all four questions is "yes," then give thanks and praise to God for His grace in your life. You can be assured you are in the faith. And if your answer is "no," then you can change that right now by going to God in prayer and confessing:

Lord,

I have taken the test—and I've failed it. I may have done all the right external things to look like a Christian. But deep down, I know now I'm not in the faith.

I haven't mourned over my sin—but now I confess my sin, I'm sorry for it, and I repent of it. I haven't hungered and thirsted for righteousness—but now I want to seek Your righteousness and serve You every day. I haven't obeyed Your Word, but today I place myself under its authority and I want to obey Your commands. I haven't loved You and others as I should, but I ask you to fill me with Your love. Come into my life, Lord, and live in me today.

In Jesus' name, Amen.

If those words are the prayer of your heart right now, then God *will* answer that prayer. . . .

And the power of positive living will begin in your life today.

THE END

Notes

Introduction

1. Jimmie C. Holland with Sheldon Lewis, *The Human Side of Cancer: Living with Hope, Coping with Uncertainty* (New York: HarperCollins, 2000).

Chapter 1

1. Benjamin Hughes, "Basketball with a Purpose," *Around Town: Stories from Charm City*, http://www.baltimorestories.com/main.cfm?nid=1&tid=290.

Chapter 3

1. Ray C. Stedman, *Letters to a Troubled Church: 1 & 2 Corinthians* (Grand Rapids: Discovery House Publishers, 2007).

Chapter 6

1. Deborah Caldwell, interview with Goldie Hawn, "Goldie: Buddhist, Jew, Jesus Freak," retrieved at http://www.beliefnet.com/story/172/story_17266_2.html.

2. C. S. Lewis, *Mere Christianity* (New York: Macmillan, 1960), p. 118.

3. Joaquim Vilà, Jordan Mitchell, "Sony: The elixir of eternal innovation," Global Technology Forum, retrieved at http://globaltechforum.eiu.com/index.asp?layout=rich_story&channelid=3&categoryid=9&doc.id=10355; Sony Global: Sony History, "The

UN Building Radio," retrieved at http://www.sony.net/Fun/SH/1-5/ h5.html; and John Nathan, "Akio Morita," TIMEasia.com, retrieved at http://www.time.com/time/asia/asia/magazine/1999/990823/morita1 .html.

Chapter 7

1. Ernest Hemingway, *The Complete Short Stories of Ernest Hemingway: The Finca Vigia Edition* (New York: Scribner, 1998), p. 29.

Chapter 8

1. Pat Williams, *Coaching Your Kids to Be Leaders: The Keys to Unlocking Their Potential* (New York: Warner Faith, 2005).

2. Jennifer Robison, "Teens Search for Role Models Close to Home," The Gallup Poll, June 10, 2003, retrieved at http://www .galluppoll.com/content/?ci=8584&pg=1.

Chapter 9

1. Ray C. Stedman, *Psalms: Folk Songs of Faith* (Grand Rapids: Discovery House Publishers, 2006).

Chapter 10

1. Billy Graham Center Archives, "A Story of the *Titanic*: Newspaper Clippings," retrieved at http://www.wheaton.edu/bgc/archives/ docs/titanic1.htm; Billy Graham Center Archives, "Article from the *Evangel*, June 1912," retrieved at http://www.wheaton.edu/bgc/ archives/docs/titanic4.htm.

Chapter 11

1. "Jane Welsh Carlyle (1801-1866): A Short Biography," retrieved at http://www.malcolmingram.com/jcbiog.htm; "Thomas Carlyle," Wikipedia, retrieved at http://en.wikipedia.org/wiki/Thomas _Carlyle.

2. Quoted by Richard De Haan in *Our Daily Bread* (July 24, 2003), and attributed to "an unknown author," retrieved at http:// www.rbc.org/odb/odb-07-24-03.shtml.

Chapter 12

1. John S. Spong, "A Call for a New Reformation," retrieved at http://www.dioceseofnewark.org/jsspong/reform.html.

2. "Edinburgh Castle," CastleXplorer.com, retrieved at http://www.castleexplorer.co.uk/scotland/Edinburgh/Edinburgh_hist.php; "Edinburgh Castle," Wikipedia, retrieved at http://en.wikipedia.org/wiki/Edinburgh_Castle; "William Kirkcaldy of Grange," Wikipedia, retrieved at http://en.wikipedia.org/wiki/William_Kirkcaldy.

Chapter 13

1. Kenneth W. Thompson, editor, *Institutions and Leadership: Prospects for the Future* (New York: University Press of America, 1987), p. 58.

Chapter 14

1. Robert Huntington Fletcher, *A History of English Literature*, e-text retrieved at http://www.gutenberg.org/dirs/etest05/7hist10.txt; and Various Authors, *Seeing Europe with Famous Authors*, Volume I, e-text retrieved at http://www.gutenberg.org/files/10588/10588.txt.

2. NMMA Awards Gallery, "1988 Hall of Fame Award recipient Ole Evinrude, 1877-1934" retrieved at http://www.nmma.org/awards/?WinnerId=79; "Ole Evinrude," retrieved at http://dalesdesigns.net/story_009.htm; Wisconsin Historical Society, "Boating in Wisconsin, a Longtime Tradition," retrieved at http://www.wisconsinhistory.org/highlights/archives/2006/07/boating_in_wisc.asp.

Chapter 15

1. Quoted by Barry Sneed and Roy Edgemon, *Transformational Discipleship* (Nashville: LifeWay Press, 1999), p. 73.

2. *The Gargoyle: The Journal of the Malcolm Muggeridge Society*, Centenary review, January 2004, retrieved on 21 June 2007 at www.malcolmmuggeridge.org/gargoyle-01-200401.pdf.

About the Author

Michael Youssef, PhD, is the founding pastor of The Church of The Apostles in Atlanta, Georgia, and the host of a worldwide radio and television program, also based in Atlanta. Dr. Youssef was educated in Australia and the United States. He and his wife have four grown children. *Leading The Way with Dr. Michael Youssef* airs on hundreds of radio and television outlets throughout North America, the United Kingdom, Australia, and New Zealand. Dr. Youssef also hosts a dual-language radio program, which translates his biblical teaching phrase by phrase from English into twenty languages that are broadcast to most of the world's population.

Discussion Questions

Introduction: **Positive *Thinking*—or Positive *Living?***

1. Can you recall a time when "positive thinking" caused you trouble or left you feeling exhausted or defeated? How did that experience affect your life and faith?

2. How would you describe the way you view your life right now:

— My circumstances are positive and my thinking is positive.

— My circumstances are positive yet I expect the worst.

— My circumstances are negative yet my thinking remains positive.

— I'm running out of hope.

— Other: _____

Explain your answer.

Chapter 1: The Inflow-Outflow Equation

1. Compare the author's description of first century Corinth with your own culture today. How does this ancient man Paul address the same challenges and temptations you face today?

2. Describe a time when you have experienced either the "inflow" or the "outflow" the author writes about.

3. Which "seas" from this chapter best describes your life right now and why?

4. Name one thing you can do this week with prayer support to experience more of God's "outflow" in your life.

Chapter 2: Claiming the Priceless Deposit

1. The author says the guarantee of salvation, purchased by Jesus on the cross, was the focus of Paul's life. What effect does this guarantee have on your life?

2. Paul suffered incredible affliction and persecution, yet his faith remained strong. If you suffered as Paul did (beatings, stonings, false imprisonment), how would your faith be impacted?

3. The author says people often attack us not because they hate us, but because they hate our gospel. Were you ever mistreated because of your stand for Christ or for biblical morality? Explain.

Chapter 3: Giving and Receiving Forgiveness

1. The author lists seven reasons to forgive others. What are they?

2. Is there someone who is difficult for you to forgive? What holds you back from forgiving? Which of the above reasons might help you to be more forgiving—and why?

3. The author says we are being led in a triumphal procession by our Commander and Chief, and our Lord's victory is certain. How do you feel about your life right now?

___ The Lord is triumphant in my life.

___ Satan, the enemy, is winning.

___ Other: _____

Explain your answer.

Chapter 4: Overcoming Timidity

1. Rate yourself on a scale of one to ten:

```
_____
 1  2  3  4  5  6  7  8  9  10
I'm very timid            I'm very bold
```

2. In what areas of your life do you need more boldness? Explain your answer.

3. The apostle Paul suggests two steps for overcoming timidity and becoming bold witnesses for Christ. What are they? How can these two steps help you witness more boldly for Christ?

Chapter 5: The Real Fountain of Youth

1. What is the secret of inner youth and vitality?

2. The author says Satan has blindfolded the eyes of many believers. What is that "blindfold"? What should you do to see life clearly?

4. Has anyone ever lied about or unfairly criticized you? How did you respond and how did your response compare with Paul's in the same situation?

Chapter 6: True Health, Wealth, and Prosperity

1. If Jesus asked you, "Who do you say I am?" what would your answer be?

2. The apostle Paul said he preferred to be away from the body and at home with the Lord. Do you identify with his view of death? Why or why not?

3. People often say, "There are many religions, but all lead to the same destination." How would you answer that statement?

4. What is one practical thing you could do this week to live as a citizen of heaven and how could your group pray for you?

Chapter 7: Mastering the Art of Peacemaking

1. How does seeing yourself as God's ambassador affect your sense of purpose and your behavior?

2. Have you ever shared the good news of Jesus Christ with another person? How did that experience change your perspective on your own problems?

3. If you never share Christ with others, what holds you back?

Chapter 8: The Power of Example

1. Name two or three people who served as examples in your life and why?

2. Name two or three people who look up to you as an example and why?

3. Have any of your heroes ever let you down and placed a "stumbling block" in your path? How did that disappointment affect your life?

4. One key to becoming an example to others is practicing the love of God. In what situations do you find it hard to love?

Chapter 9: Sorrow: The Back Door to Happiness

1. The author says there are two ways to deal with sorrow—and both involve pain. Describe them in your own words. Which do you tend to use?

2. Can you forgive without reconciling with that person? Why or why not?

3. In your own words, what's the difference between godly sorrow and worldly sorrow? Give examples of each.

4. How can godly sorrow restore any broken relationships in your life?

Chapter 10: Getting Through Giving

1. Imagine giving up everything you have to make your next-door neighbor rich. Would you do that? Paul wrote that Jesus became poor to make us rich. How does this realization affect your life?

2. Have you ever tried to manipulate God into blessing you? What was wrong with your attitude? What should your attitude be?

3. What does it mean to be an heir of God? How does this great truth affect the way you live your life?

Chapter 11: Being Appreciated

1. Share a time when appreciation made a difference in your life.

2. Share a time in your life when giving made you feel "hilarious."

3. Describe a time in your life when God provided for you beyond all your expectations. How did that experience impact your faith?

4. Describe a time when God answered your prayers in an unexpected way. What did you feel at that time?

Chapter 12: When Pride Is Good

1. The author says the only cure for sinful pride is to daily express our utter dependence on God. List three blessings you've received from God you cannot take credit for.

2. The author talks about a "pride you can be proud of" In your own words, what is holy, healthy pride?

3. Name a person you greatly admire. What is one thing that person does to build people up?

4. When you think of persistence in the face of opposition, who comes to mind and why?

Chapter 13: When Jealousy Is a Virtue

1. The Bible says God is a "jealous" God. Does that description sound positive or negative to you? Explain your answer.

2. The author draws a distinction between jealousy and envy. Re-state that distinction in your own words. If possible, give examples.

4. Are you excited about the prospect of spending eternity with Jesus? Why or why not?

6. If you know of a fellow Christian who is caught in a sin, how should you act?

Chapter 14: Stars Instead of Scars

1. Do you believe you have a "thorn in the flesh" right now? If you feel comfortable talking about it, please explain.

2. Have you ever prayed for God to remove some suffering from your life? What resulted and how do you feel about that?

Chapter 15: Ready for the Exam

1. The apostle Paul tells us to examine ourselves to see if we are in the faith. The author says that when we take this exam, it's a case of, "Heads you win–tails you win!" Explain in your own words what this means.

2. The author suggests four questions we should ask ourselves:

Question 1: "Am I eager to confess my sins and seek forgiveness?"

Question 2: "Do I hunger and thirst for righteousness?"

Question 3: "Do I submit myself to the authority of God's Word?"

Question 4: "Do I genuinely love God and others?"

Which of these questions is the hardest for you? Explain.

*   *   *   *   *

Ask your discussion group friends to pray for you and check in with you as you grow in your faith and Christian maturity. The power of positive living begins in your life right now!